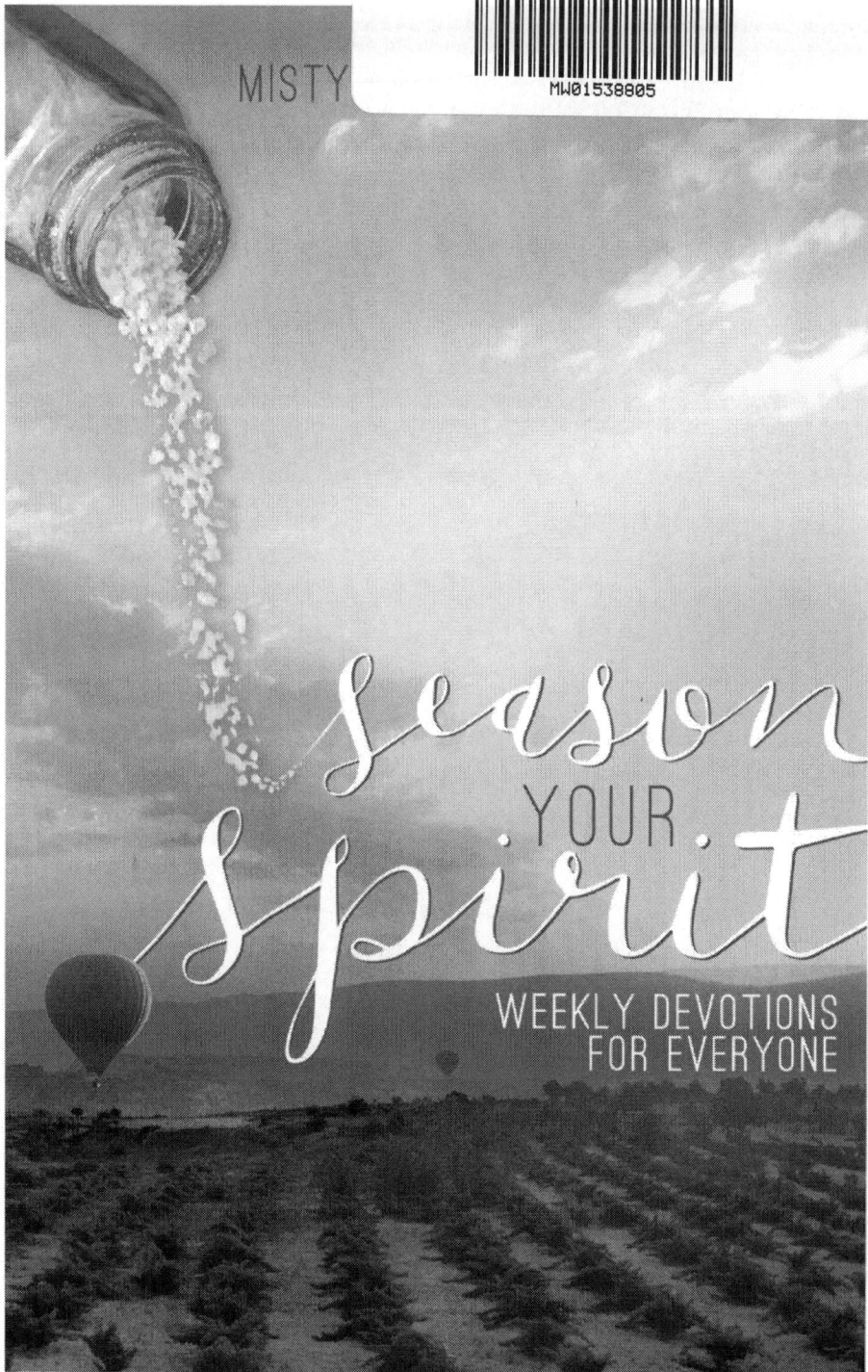

MISTY

season
YOUR
spirit

WEEKLY DEVOTIONS
FOR EVERYONE

MISTY NOVAK + DEBBY BERRY

season YOUR spirit

WEEKLY DEVOTIONS
FOR EVERYONE

Season Your Spirit: Weekly Devotions for Everyone

Copyright © 2015 by Misty Novak and Debra Berry

All Rights Reserved.

Cover design by Abby Beard

www.abbybeard.com

The Scripture quotations contained herein are from:

The **King James Version Bible (KJV)** was authorized by King James I and is sometimes referred to as the "Authorized Version". It was translated by the Church of England and was first published in 1611.

The **New Revised Standard Version Bible with the Apocrypha (NRSA)**, copyright 1989, Division of Christian Education of the National Council of the Churches of Christ in the United States of America. Used by permission. All rights reserved.

Canada Dry and the shield design are registered trademarks with ® Dr. Pepper/7-Up Inc.

The game **Cranium™** is a registered trademark to Hasbro games. Hasbro and all related terms are trademarks of Hasbro.

Father Knows Best copyright © 1954-1963 A Rodney / Young Production

Girl Scouts™ is a registered trademark of Girls Scouts of the United States of America, a 501 (c)(3) Organization.

iPhone™ is a registered trademark with Apple, Inc.

The movie, **Karate Kid™** and all its rights are registered to Filmmakers on IMDbPro.

Make Way For Ducklings copyright ©1941(renewed 1969) by Robert McCloskey by The Viking Press.

Miracle on 34th Street™ 1947-1974 THX is a trademark of LucasFilm, LTD.

Motrin™ has a registered trademark with ®McNEIL-PPC, Inc.

Sugar Bear™ and Sugar Crisp are registered trademarks with Post Foods, LLC.

The Three Billy Goats Gruff copyright ©1973 by Clarion Books a Houghton Mifflin Company imprint; copyright ©1987 by Janet Stevens; and copyright ©1983 by Ellen Appleby by Scholastic, Inc.

Tums™ has a registered trademark with ®TUMS.

The book and stuffed toys of **Winnie the Pooh™** are registered trademarks of Disney.

The device called **UP™** has a registered trademark with Jawbone™.

For Our Families

We love you all and praise the Lord

for our time together.

Our parents:

Bob & Ellen Ward

Our husbands:

Dan Novak & Ervin Berry

Our children and their spouses:

David Sturgeon

Zachary Novak (in spirit)

Joel & Hillary Novak

Brytni (Novak) & Jason Hessler

Stephen & Leah Berry

Our grandchildren:

Camden & Kendall Novak

Lily & Connor Hessler

Chloe, Ethan & Gage Berry

Acknowledgements

Thank You...

Most Gracious and Loving God, our Savior, Jesus Christ and the Holy Spirit, for the gift of your unfailing love and peace throughout our lives. Thank you for the gift of eternal life. Without You, we are nothing.

Our Family and Friends, for being a part of our lives. Thank you for our time together, memories, and the love we share.

Our Editor and Friend, Elmore Hammes, for sharing your skills and talents with us. Your tireless support and professional assurance made this book a reality.

TABLE OF CONTENTS

Added Spice

Extra Devotionals to be used, as needed, for months that have 5 weeks

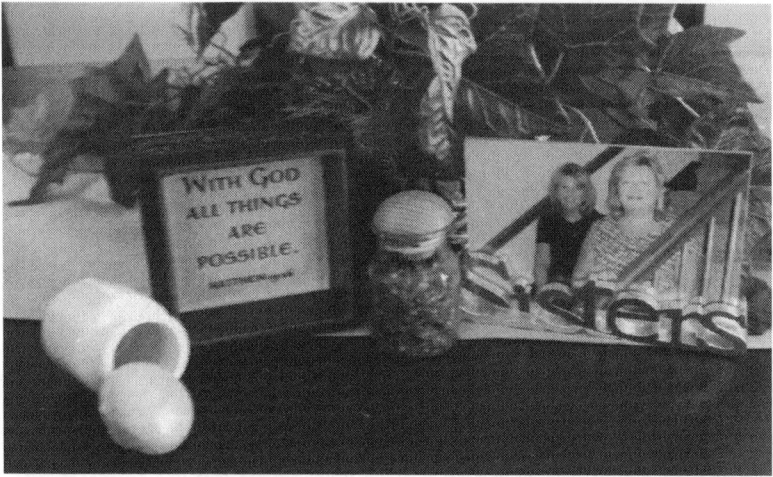

Introduction

Season Your Spirit...

Have you ever tasted anything that has not been seasoned? Because it lacks flavor, you don't want to eat it. If the food has great flavor, you savor it. All of us need to feed our spirits and add spice to our lives. If you nourish your spiritual life, you can fill up with the heavenly cooking from God.

Season Your Spirit allows you to pause and reflect on scripture linked to a personal story with photographs. Questions are provided to allow you, individually or in a small group, to sift through the ingredients of your life. Some blending may be needed as you filter through the portions provided. The challenge points following each story will help you enrich your spirit in order to face the ordeals and blessings in your life.

The word "season" takes on another meaning in Indiana. The Midwest provides the opportunity to relish Winter, Spring, Summer, and Fall. This book walks with you through reflections of a few seasonal experiences. When seasons change, you can feel something inside shift in unison. The Lord can stir within us, helping us grow and change, just like the seasons.

Our reason for including scriptures from both Catholic and Protestant Bibles is to be more ecumenical. As you read this book, may your heart and soul be refreshed and your spirit seasoned with new revitalized flavor. Life is an unfinished dish with the Holy Spirit as the chef. Join with us and add just the right spices to become the "Best Version of Yourselves."

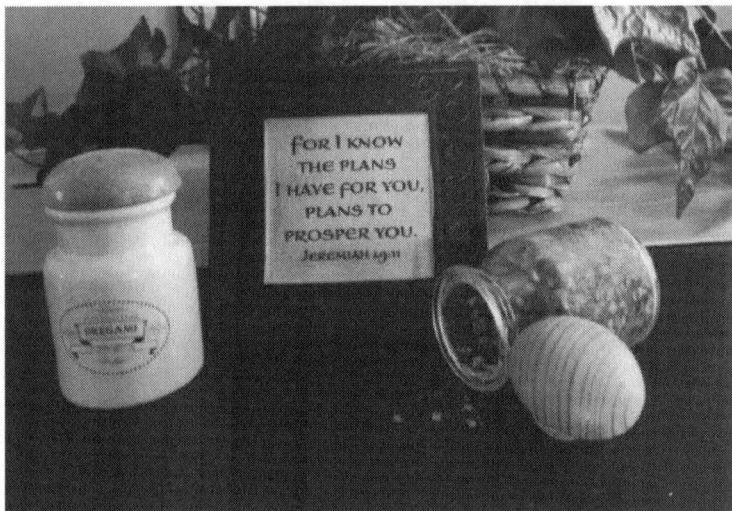

4

January

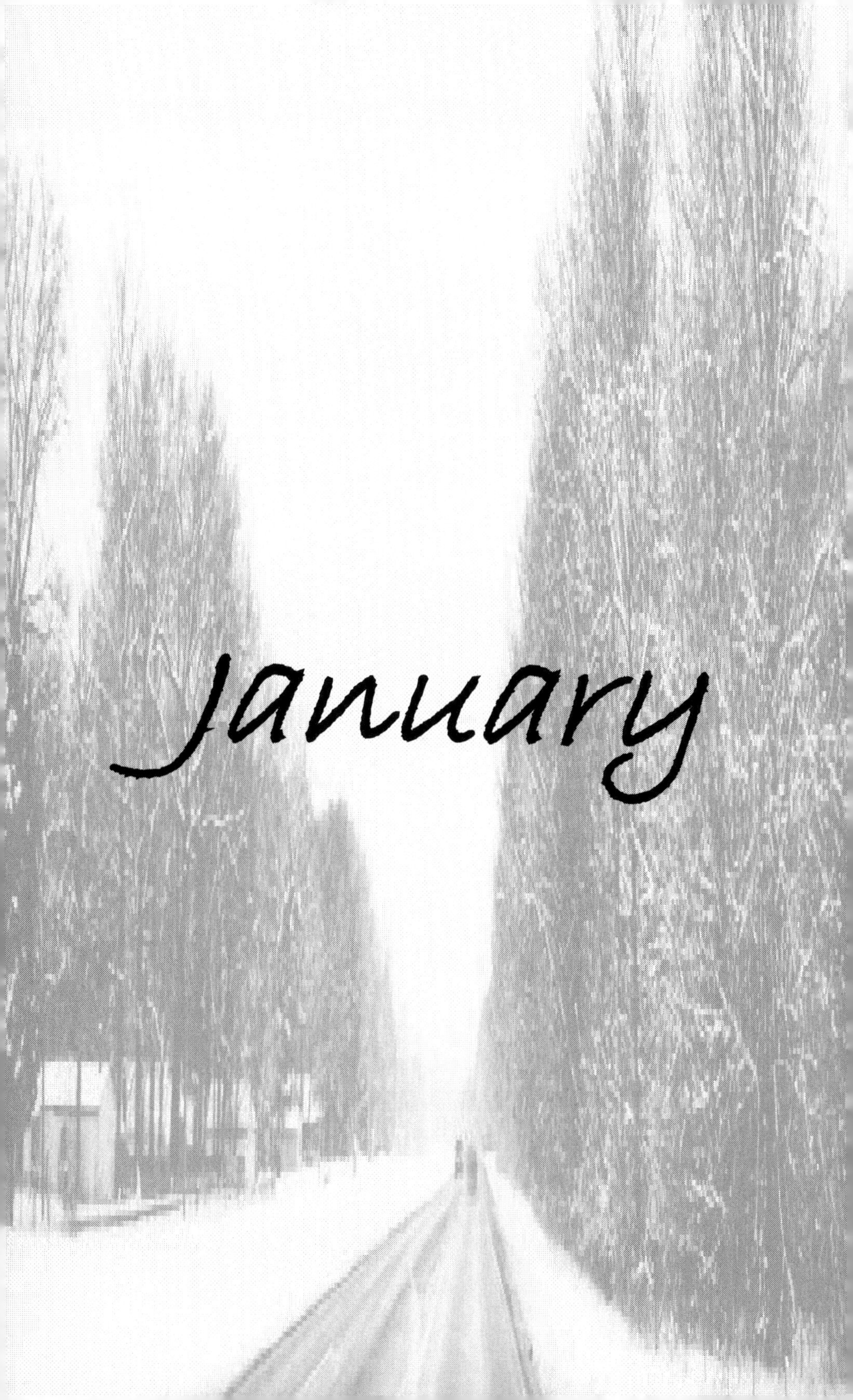

Hebrews 11:3

NRSA
By faith we understand that the worlds were prepared by the word of God, so that what is seen was made from things that are not visible.

KJV
Through faith we understand that the worlds were framed by the word of God, so that things which are seen were not made of things which do appear.

"The Miracle of Santa"

The season of Christmas has come and gone. All the bows, ribbons and wrappings tossed aside while decorations and heirlooms are boxed and put away until next Christmas rolls around again. It's a lot of work for one day—but what a day it is! Celebrating the birth of our Lord is worth so much more than, as some would say, "the fuss." It's a season of miracles!

I love watching all the Christmas movies, but I have to say I have a few favorites. *Miracle on 34th Street* ranks among them. It's all about whether or not Santa is a real person. One of the characters, Fred Gailey, makes a statement that has always reminded me of something from the Bible. He states, "Faith is believing when common sense tells you not to."

Santa possesses so many admirable characteristics: Laughter, fun, happiness, giving and thinking of others more than himself—doesn't this person sound like someone you'd want to be like? As Kris Kringle says, "Oh, Christmas isn't just a day, it's a frame of mind. Seems we're all so busy trying to beat the other fellow in making things go faster and look shinier and cost less that Christmas and I are sort of getting lost in the shuffle." I must confess that I have been caught up in the shuffle and lost sight of the truth behind the season.

The New Year calls us to be better versions of ourselves, more like Kris Kringle, aka Santa Claus. My husband, Dan, had the opportunity to portray Santa one year. Ironically, he hung the suit on our elliptical machine. I don't think of Santa and an exercise machine going together, but if Santa wants to be a better version of himself, well...maybe, just maybe, Dan didn't hang it in a strange place.

Sometimes when I am feeling low or lose sight of what is real, I find myself echoing the thoughts of the little girl in the movie, Susan, who repeats the phrase, "I believe... I believe... It's silly, but I believe." Let's all believe and take on the New Year's challenge to keep on the suit of the season, exercise those attributes inside all of us and become a better version of ourselves...more like Kris Kringle!

7

Points to Ponder

➤ What characteristics of Kris Kringle do you possess? (e.g. laughter, fun, happiness, giving and thinking of others more than himself)

➤ Assessing your faith, do *you* believe when common sense tells you not to?

➤ How can you be the best version of yourself?

➤ What do you think the quote from the movie, *Miracle on 34th Street* means: "Christmas isn't just a day, it's a frame of mind"?

➤ Describe the miracles you have witnessed.

Challenge Yourself

❖ Strive to be more faithful.

❖ Look for the miracles.

❖ Aim to be the best version of yourself.

❖ ADD YOUR OWN CHALLENGE

Matthew 6:9-13

NRSA

9 "Pray then in this way: Our Father in heaven, hallowed be your name. 10 Your kingdom come. Your will be done, on earth as it is in heaven. 11 Give us this day our daily bread. 12 And forgive us our debts, as we also have forgiven our debtors. 13 And do not bring us to the time of trial, but rescue us from the evil one.

KJV

9 After this manner therefore pray ye: Our Father which art in heaven, Hallowed be thy name. 10 Thy kingdom come. Thy will be done in earth, as it is in heaven. 11 Give us this day our daily bread. 12 And forgive us our debts, as we forgive our debtors. 13 And lead us not into temptation, but deliver us from evil: For thine is the kingdom, and the power, and the glory, forever. Amen.

"One is Silver and the Other's Gold"

Friendship is a valuable piece of my life. I have friends who have cried with me through extraordinarily rough times and have laughed with me in cheerful, fun times. True friends forgive my weaknesses and celebrate my successes. Friends are those rare people who ask how we are and really want to know the answer.

I recall spending time with an old friend from high school that I hadn't seen in thirty years. Even though we weren't close, it was like we hadn't missed a beat. Time melted the years and the wrinkles away.

Lives touch other lives and past friends continue into the present. Sometimes old wounds can fester and leave scars. If we offend or have been offended, The Lord's Prayer states, "Forgive us our trespasses, as we forgive those that trespass against us." Friends do just that.

We all make mistakes, and often that can cause pain. As the famous reggae singer Bob Marley said, "The truth is... everyone is going to hurt you. You just got to find the ones worth suffering for."

Friends keep us balanced, filling the scales with light and heavy memories. There was a song I learned in Girl Scouts about making new friends, but keeping the old: "One is silver and the other's gold." Hopefully, we can all strive to be a friend of worth and value.

Points to Ponder

➢ What is your definition of a friend?

➢ What makes some friends forgive your weaknesses and celebrate your successes while others don't?

➢ Do you need friends? Why or why not?

➢ Describe the difference between a *silver* friend and a *gold* friend.

➢ What kind of friend are you? For example, do you ask how your friend is, but then don't care about the answer?

Challenge Yourself

❖ When you ask your friend how they are, listen for the answer.

❖ Be the kind of friend you want to have.

❖ Evaluate your friends and keep only the good ones.

❖ ADD YOUR OWN CHALLENGE

January—Week 3

Matthew 11:28

NRSA
Come to me, all you who are weary and find life burdensome, and I will refresh you.

KJV
Come unto me, all ye that labour and are heavy laden, and I will give you rest.

"A Snowy Road"

The snow keeps coming without an end in sight. I continue to drive onward—down the road. All this snow and bitter cold wind calls me toward the comforts of home where it's safe and warm—the place where I can just be me.

In between snow falls, when the sun does come out, the white blanket reflects its light but the temperature and the frigid air tell another story.

Hope is at the core of the weather—hope of warmth and shorter distances to travel. Hope that when my spirit feels frozen by problems and strife, I'll dig through life's drifts to find my way home, the place to warm my soul.

I can't help but think of the last phrase, written by American writer, Robert Frost, about a snowy road much like this one:

The woods are lovely, dark and deep

But I have promises to keep

And miles to go before I sleep

And miles to go before I sleep

Those well-known words echo a timeless message that rings true for me.

Points to Ponder

➢ Do you find home a place of comfort?

➢ Where and with whom can you just be yourself?

➢ When you feel overwhelmed, do you seek the comfort of others or do you prefer the solace of being alone?

➢ What brings you hope?

➢ Re-read the last phrase of Robert Frost's poem. What represents the woods in your life?

Challenge Yourself

❖ Let Jesus carry your burdens.

❖ When discouraged, don't despair, pray for someone else in need.

❖ Spend some time talking to God.

❖ ADD YOUR OWN CHALLENGE

Matthew 13:47

NRSA
Again, the kingdom of heaven is like a net that was thrown into the sea and caught fish of every kind;

KJV
Again, the kingdom of heaven is like unto a net, that was cast into the sea, and gathered of every kind:

"Icy Fishing"

Cold is not something I embrace willingly. In fact, my husband would say that I announce my lack of regard for the cold rather vocally. Rock Lake, where our family cottage is located, is popular for fishing, even in the winter. Just the thought of sitting in an ice hut on a frozen lake makes me shiver.

I can picture it easily. The pier of the lake cottage reveals the coldness of the water. Ice forms on the edges surrounding the lake, and then freezes solid. The sky is an ominous shade of gray. Snow lies on the banks giving the lake an even colder dimension. Brrrrrr!

In the spring, summer, and fall, I love to fish. The peacefulness of the lake, the rocking of the boat, and the anticipation of the bobber going under, all of these things factor into why I enjoy the sport. I thought about those winter fishermen and their determination. How could they sit in an ice hut just waiting for the fish to bite? Could my love for fishing ever outweigh my aversion to the cold? Perhaps, with toe-heaters, hand-warmers and a thermos of hot tea, I might tackle the cold for the sport.

American author Washington Irving once said, "There is certainly something in angling that tends to produce a serenity of the mind." Life is a conundrum of events. We make choices based on many things. Sometimes you have to make the decision to push through adversity to find your joy—to find what brings happiness.

God is our shelter in the cold, our port in life's icy waters. It's up to us to persevere to reach what gives us that peace—that serenity of the mind.

Points to Ponder

➢ In the scripture, how is heaven like a net thrown into the sea? What does "every kind" mean?

➢ What temperatures or situations make you uncomfortable?

➢ What *icy waters* have frozen your life?

➢ How has your faith pulled you out of those waters?

➢ Where do you find your serenity of the mind?

Challenge Yourself

❖ Work to throw out your heavenly net.

❖ Anticipate good things.

❖ Catch others doing "good" and tell them.

❖ ADD YOUR OWN CHALLENGE

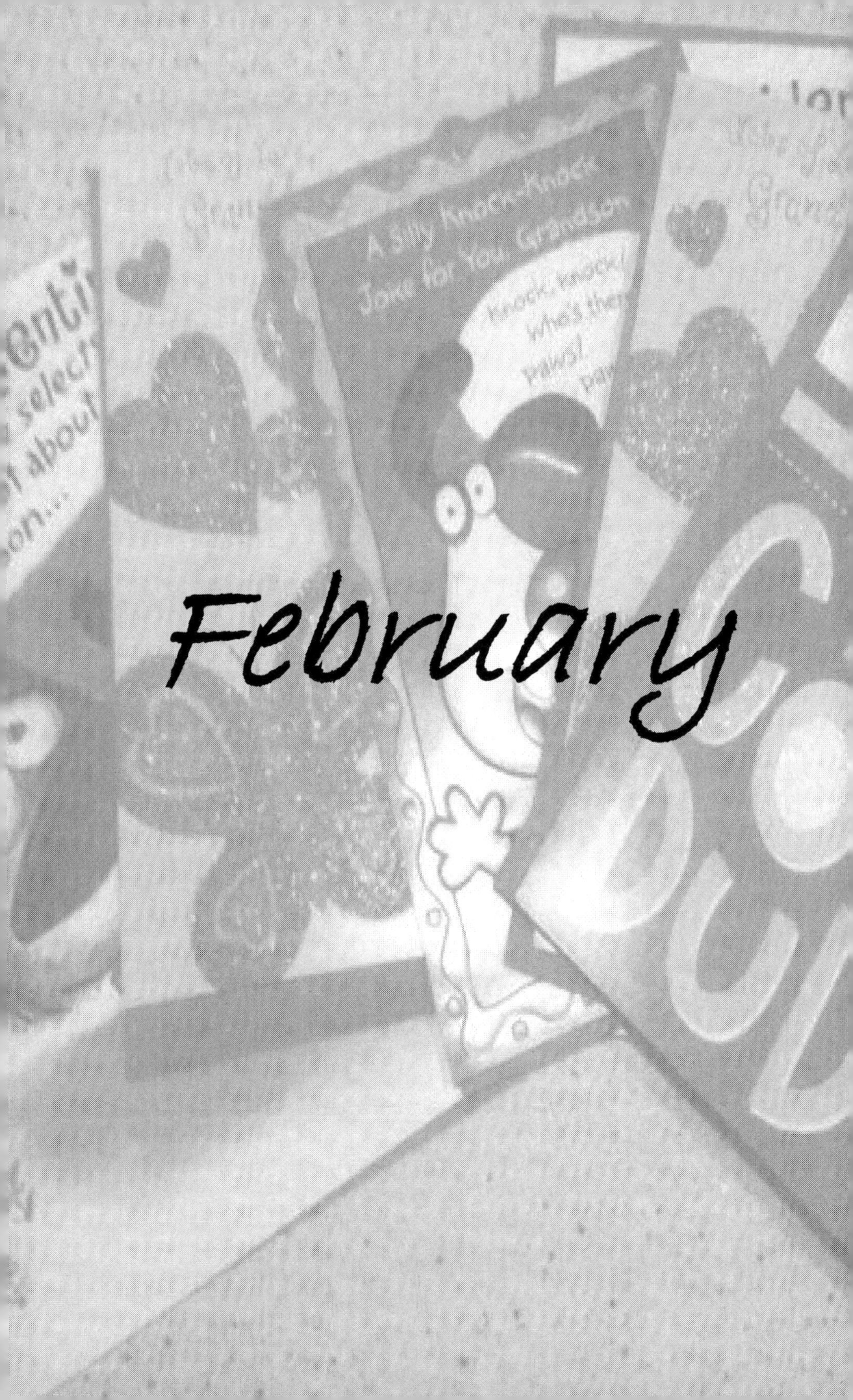

February

1 Thessalonians 4:9

NRSA
Now concerning love of the brothers and sisters, you do not need to have anyone write to you, for you yourselves have been taught by God to love one another;

KJV
But as touching brotherly love ye need not that I write unto you: for ye yourselves are taught of God to love one another.

"Love is All You Need"

Not too long ago, The Beatles celebrated the 50th anniversary of their début on The Ed Sullivan Show. Yes, I am old enough to remember that night. Like most young girls, I was glued to the television and sang right along with them. I shook my hair and longed to hold their hand.

The Beatles repertoire lives on today. A vast number of their songs are about love. Many of their lyrics are quoted between friends and those who are more than friends. One particular phrase from a song has stayed with me over the years: "All you need is love." In the midst of all the turmoil and strife in our lives, I'd like to believe that love really is all we need. Love holds the key to good memories and warm thoughts. It gives us pause to close our eyes and feel the warmth of a hug and picture love shining in a smile. Love fills the niche and gives a reason to return the love. Mother Teresa said, "Let us always meet each other with smile, for the smile is the beginning of love."

Let's all smile and give out some love today and every day because love is all you need—yeah, yeah, yeah!

Points to Ponder

➤ Remembering back to your youth, describe a fond memory of something or someone you loved.

➤ How do you know you are loved?

➤ How loving are you toward others?

➤ Do you take Mother Teresa's advice by greeting everyone (strangers too) with a smile? Re-read the scripture and discuss how you apply it to your life. Why do you smile at others?

➤ How do you feel when that smile you give to another is not given in return?

Challenge Yourself

❖ Make it a point to greet others with a smile.

❖ Be sure to show love towards others in a variety of ways (i.e. hugs, notes, small tokens).

❖ ADD YOUR OWN CHALLENGE

February—Week 2

1 Peter 4:8

NRSA
Above all, maintain constant love for one another, for love covers a multitude of sins.

KJV
And above all things have fervent charity among yourselves; for charity shall cover the multitude of sins.

"More than Just a Card"

February has been the month to celebrate love dating way back to the Middle Ages. In fact, Valentine's Day ranks second only to Christmas in the number of greeting cards sent. Cards have always been special to me so I guess that's why I still enjoy the holiday.

As a kid, I loved Valentine's Day. During elementary school, each year our homework assignment was to decorate a box for our classroom party. Most years, I used an old shoe box. Red or pink construction paper or tissue paper covered the outside. Hand crafted hearts of various sizes and colors adorned the top and sides. The lid was wrapped separately so the valentines could be removed without destroying the beautiful box.

Decorating the box was fun, but after the Valentine's Day party, we would get to open those note cards of love. I would open the larger cards last because I just knew they were from someone special.

Upon returning home, I'd re-open the box and line up the cards, taking my time to enjoy each one. If I received one in the mail, I felt extra special. A mailed card still remains a special treat.

Now that the grandkids are starting to read, the message in the card is more important than ever. It must be simple but clearly state our love. For the past few years, I gave the grandchildren their valentines personally so I could watch their faces light up. Now that they are older, I mail the cards hoping they will feel special, too.

We can use a touch of Valentine's Day throughout the year. A card can lift you out of a bad mood and elevate your

spirit, sending a message of love and caring. One of my favorite authors, Anonymous, once said, "Valentine hearts beat more passionately than everyday hearts." It's up to us to pick up that beat on more than just this designated day of love.

Points to Ponder

➤ What are your memories of Valentine's Day?

➤ If you sent Jesus a Valentine, what would it say?

➤ If you could send a card to anyone, living or not, who would it be and what would you say?

➤ Do you believe that love conquers all and can overcome all sin?

➤ Did you know that Biblically, charity and love mean the same thing? Does this change your view of charitable organizations?

Challenge Yourself

❖ Send a card to someone who might need some love.

❖ Think of a charitable organization you want to be involved in and act on it.

❖ ADD YOUR OWN CHALLENGE

February—Week 3

Ecclesiastes 11:9

NRSA
Rejoice, young man, while you are young, and let your heart cheer you in the days of your youth. Follow the inclination of your heart and the desire of your eyes, but know that for all these things God will bring you into judgment.

KJV
Rejoice, O young man, in thy youth; and let thy heart cheer thee in the days of thy youth, and walk in the ways of thine heart, and in the sight of thine eyes: but know thou, that for all these things God will bring thee into judgment.

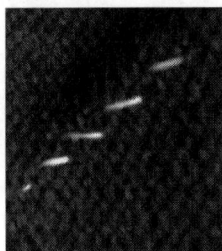

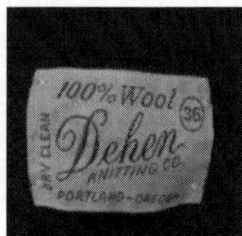

"Something to Cheer About"

Although I'm retired, I have occasionally been asked to do testing for the school system. One Friday, it was spirit day. Teachers were asked to support the cause by wearing school colors from any of the three high schools that were once thriving in our city. My mind raced back to my high school days.

High school seems like a separate lifetime. Some thoughts are clear but many are just blurred memories. When I walked out of high school, I was sure that contact with a lot of classmates would be lost. After all, my graduating class was more than 400, but hoped that some friends would remain forever. Certainly the building would always be there—who would have thought differently? Well, Madison Heights closed in 1997, due to increasing costs and declining enrollment. A city that once housed three high schools was consolidated into one, and Madison Heights was no more. Sadly, it seemed that part of my heritage was lost.

After a day of testing students, I went through my cedar chest and pulled out my 42-year-old cheerleading sweater. It still looked the same as the day I packed it away. The sweater is 100% wool. I began to think about modern clothing. How many garments today are made of anything as durable as wool? How many could stand the test of time?

I turned the sweater inside out and examined the stitching. I remember watching my mom hand-stitch the large white-trimmed letter onto the black V-neck sweater. She had to use an upholstery needle to do the job. Each stitch was spaced accordingly to hold the letter in place. As I ran my fingers across the large letter "M", thoughts of my friends and days-gone-by filled my mind. Many friends and even family were tied to that sweater.

Over the years, I have reconnected with several old high school friends. Some of us keep in touch through Facebook™. My old sweater represents things that last. Friends are each stitch carefully placed to hold us together. Our friendship is like 100% wool, strong enough to stand the test of time. We have aged and gone our own ways, but we came together to cheer each other on through the highs and lows in our lives. I recall Principal Robert Collier coining the phrase "Walk Tall—Be Proud—You are a Pirate." Our friendships are something to cheer about—something that lasts beyond a building. Friends—caring and cheering each other, telling them to walk tall and remember we are not alone!

Points to Ponder

➢ Have things you cheered about when you were young remained important to you or have they changed?

➢ Name something that has endured the test of time.

➢ Are you like the wool in the sweater giving 100% of yourself to Jesus?

➢ In your spiritual life, what makes you cheer?

Challenge Yourself

❖ Send some cheerful words to someone or phone a friend.

❖ Strive to give 100% of yourself to Jesus.

❖ Cheer on your friends.

❖ ADD YOUR OWN CHALLENGE

February—Week 4

Ephesians 5:15-17

NRSA

15 Be careful then how you live, not as unwise people but as wise, 16 making the most of the time, because the days are evil. 17 So do not be foolish, but understand what the will of the Lord is.

KJV

15 See then that ye walk circumspectly, not as fools, but as wise, 16 redeeming the time, because the days are evil. 17 Wherefore be ye not unwise, but understanding what the will of the Lord is.

"Pockets of Time"

While at a wedding reception, I spotted a most unusual sight. There, hanging strategically over our heads were huge hanging pocket watches, each showing a different time! The sight was amazing and the mere spectacle of these time pieces had me thinking of time being suspended in midair. Wouldn't it be great to have time stand still for a while—or to carry time in your pocket like loose change?

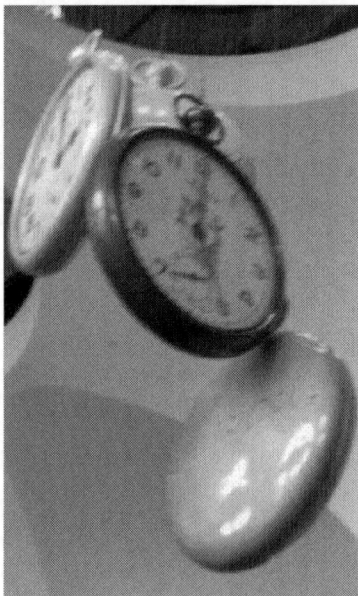

When I was first married, I bought my husband a pocket watch. For me, pocket watches possess an aura of elegance and class of days gone by. My grandpa had a pocket watch and I always loved how he would take it out, push the button to pop open the ornately etched cover and tell me the time. Then I watched my husband re-enact the same process with his watch. I love both these men, and it was wonderful to see Dan mirroring Grandpa, one generation following another.

Time is an investment. As Abraham Lincoln once said, "Nothing valuable can be lost by taking time." Time is an intangible part of life. I reflected on those suspended pocket watches, frozen on different times, thinking our memories are similar, serving as placeholders in our lives. Precious as memories are, it is best if we keep our time moving forward, remembering to use it wisely.

Points to Ponder

➢ Name a particular activity that actually took you some length of time to participate in or complete.

➢ Some people plan their day down to the minute. Do you plan your day? Why or why not?

➢ I have heard it said, "There are just not enough hours in the day." What does this mean? Have you said this?

➢ Recall and describe an event when you believe you wasted time.

➢ How much time do you invest in God each day?

Challenge Yourself

❖ Begin your day investing time with God.

❖ Take as much time as you need in a particular activity.

❖ Be careful not to waste away the minutes, but to make time count.

❖ ADD YOUR OWN CHALLENGE

March

Psalm 77:19

NRSA
Your way was through the sea, your path, through the mighty waters; yet your footprints were unseen.

KJV
Thy way is in the sea, and thy path in the great waters, and thy footsteps are not known.

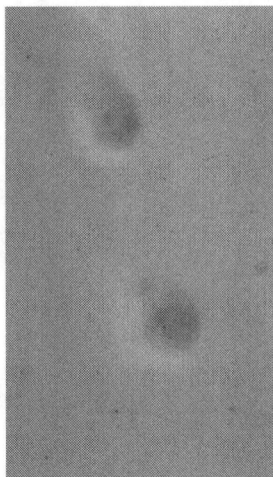

"Tracks"

How can you tell where you have been? In the winter, snow will reveal imprints left by whatever creature has traveled through the cold, white stuff. Occasionally, I have even seen coyote footprints right outside our front door. I have to admit I was not too excited to see those impressions. The paw prints revealed a straight path of determined purpose.

In our backyard, two of our grandkids, Lily and Connor, played in the snow with their new puppy, Penny. Their footprints were scattered in various directions. An unclear and uncharted course was displayed in those footprints. Some of their tracks intersected and even ran together—no end in sight!

Sand, too, reflects whatever has traveled through it. While visiting my parents in sunny, warm Florida, I had the chance to witness this first hand. There is a strip of beach not highly traveled. As I walked that stretch of beach, I made a path near the water's edge. Then, turning back, I took a picture of my trail and waited for what I knew would happen next. Within a few minutes, the waves totally swept away most of my footprints. The deepest print faded last. Eventually, every trace that I had been there vanished.

Sand and snow are two different substances, but do have a commonality. Even though one is found in warm climate and the other in extreme cold, they both have the ability to give you an idea about who has passed through them. Both are soft so that the trail will eventually fade away.

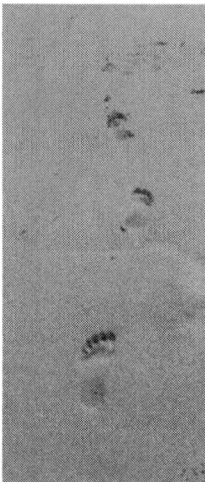

We all make tracks. What will we leave behind? Will we leave an unclear print or one that is deep and lingering? Will our path be straight or jumbled? An unknown author once said, "We all leave footprints in the sand, the question is, will we be a big heel, or a great soul." No matter what the climate is in our lives, we all will leave some sort of impression on someone. It's up to us to be sure-footed enough to leave a good path—one that won't vanish.

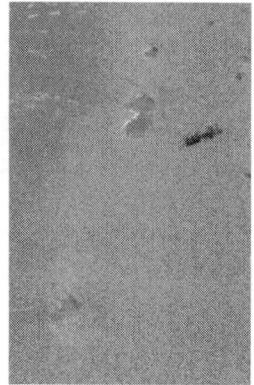

Points to Ponder

➤ Has anything in your past left you feeling trampled down? Describe.

➤ What do you think of when you see footprints in the sand or snow?

➤ The word *impression* has a double meaning in this story. Your footprints leave an impression in the sand and snow; however, you leave an impression on people and likewise, others leave an impression on you. Is the impression you leave on others a positive one? How do you know?

➤ In reading the scripture, what is the meaning of "your footprints are unseen"?

Challenge Yourself

❖ Be conscious of the impression you leave on others.

❖ Do not be quick to judge others and their first impression they leave upon you.

❖ ADD YOUR OWN CHALLENGE

March—Week 2

1 Corinthians 11:34

NRSA
If you are hungry, eat at home, so that when you come together, it will not be for your condemnation. About the other things I will give instructions when I come.

KJV
And if any man hunger, let him eat at home; that ye come not together unto condemnation. And the rest will I set in order when I come.

"You Can Always Go Home"

Tuesdays are Terrific for me or at least that's what the grandkids and I have taken to calling this particular day of the week. After marrying, our own children landed near enough that Tuesday evenings has become a permanent babysitting time for Dan and me. What a true blessing to have our house full of dancing, romping, and lots of giggling—mostly from Dan and me.

One Tuesday, all four, freshly bathed and shampooed grandkids and I sat on the sofa, immersed in reading *The Three Billy Goats Gruff*. Our daughter Brytni bounded through the door, returning from her workout, glistening with sweat. She went to the kitchen, filled up her glass at our water cooler, then proceeded to look over the contents of the refrigerator. She quickly came across her favorite vegetable, green beans. "Hey, Mom, are you guys saving these for later or can I have them?"

I glanced up from the book and past the island separating the family room from the kitchen. "No, go ahead," I responded briefly then continued reading.

"Great! I am starved!" Brytni exclaimed as she quickly shoved them into the microwave to await that "ding" before wolfing them down. While she was waiting, Brytni casually went through the pantry and other cabinets looking for other food options. We, of course, remained engrossed in the Troll and goats' activities in the story.

Meanwhile, our just-got-off-work son, Joel emerged onto the scene. "Hi guys! Looks like you are having fun," he proclaimed. Without so much as a blink, he maneuvered through the kitchen in much the same fashion as his little sister. The refrigerator or the pantry always seem to be the top places to graze (the term seems fitting because of the goats in the story were involved in the same activity). Upon opening the "fridge," he pulled out a plate and inquired, "Hey, when did you get this Pizza King™ pizza?" all the while he was shoving a cold piece into his mouth.

Pausing from the story, I had to chuckle at the scene being played in the kitchen. "Are you two hungry or what?"

Both of the grown children, now in their early thirties, looked at each other and giggled, then back to me. Joel paused before continuing his quest for more food treasures, proclaiming, "Hey, it's always great to come home!"

It's funny how some things never change. I'm lucky that my teenagers-now-grown are still foraging in our fridge!

Points to Ponder

➤ Do you think that you can always go home?

➤ Where do you feel comfortable enough to open the refrigerator or pantry?

➤ What feeds your spirit?

➤ Have you fed your family spiritually? How?

➤ What do you think Jesus meant in this scripture when He said "...eat at home..."?

Challenge Yourself

❖ Take some time to feed your spirit.

❖ Pray for your family.

❖ Work on making your home a welcoming place.

❖ ADD YOUR OWN CHALLENGE

March—Week 3

Job 12:7

NRSA
But ask the animals, and they will teach you; the birds of the air, and they will tell you;

KJV
But ask now the beasts, and they shall teach thee; and the fowls of the air, and they shall tell thee:

"Songs of Spring"

Some time ago, my husband, Dan and I spotted a beautiful bright red cardinal singing outside of our bedroom window. Cardinals don't migrate, so we have enjoyed watching them through the winter. Their color is breathtaking in winter's snowy backyards although it's the most fun for us to watch them in the spring.

Other birds joined in the chorus but that male cardinal was the most vociferous. He was relentless about calling to his mate. His loud, metallic chip note made the cardinal's song easy to identify. The female cardinal is one of the few female birds to sing and she often sings while sitting on the nest. I love to hear them calling to each other!

With all that being said, this pair of song birds had given me hope that this never ending, record breaking winter would come to a close. The snow would melt and warm weather would be coming.

If troubles and cold thoughts drift through your life, take a few moments, pause and listen to the music coming from the trees. Close your eyes, envision the sights and sounds announcing that there is a change of seasons. Let your troubles melt away. Sing a song of spring just like the cardinals!

Points to Ponder

➢ Describe how weather or a season can change your mood.

➢ What can you learn from the cardinals?

➢ What do you think Job meant by this scripture?

➢ Does nature speak to your spirit? How?

Challenge Yourself

❖ Take a few minutes to listen to nature's sounds. Write them down.

❖ Look out your window and be positive, regardless of what you see.

❖ ADD YOUR OWN CHALLENGE

Ecclesiastes 3:1

NRSA

For everything there is a season, and a time for every matter under heaven:

KJV

To every thing there is a season, and a time to every purpose under the heaven:

"Give It Some Time"

Have you ever felt as if the day would never end or you'd never survive an incident—or a season? Winters in Indiana seem never ending. Will the snow ever melt? Is it always going to be gray and gloomy? Don't get me wrong, I love snow and the changing seasons. Let me just say, I have been ready for the snow to go.

My husband, Dan and I love to hike at Mounds State Park near our home. The path takes us to the river where troubles seem to float away. One week, an abundance of snow had fallen and the trek was difficult. Snow drifted over my boot tops. My steps were more marching than walking, but it was worth the trip. The view was as picturesque as a postcard. Even though it was beautiful, I longed for spring. I wanted the trees to bud, the birds to sing, and the spring colors to wash away that winter gray.

What a difference time makes! A week later, Dan and I took the same path and all that snow had almost disappeared! The trees were bursting with songs. Yes, spring was in the air! The landscape was transformed.

Life is a series of events—some good and some that weigh us down. If we let the bad stuff swallow us up, then the devil has won. As I gazed at the pictures from one week to another, I thought about what a difference time had made. We should take heart in the words of poet Anne Bradstreet: "If we had no winter, the spring would not be so pleasant: if we did not sometimes taste of adversity, prosperity would not be so welcome."

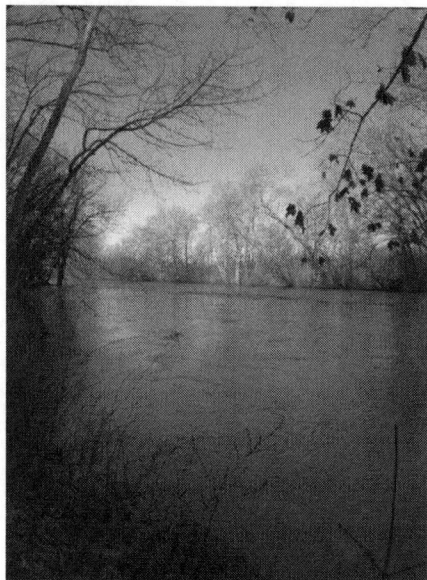

Points to Ponder

➢ Which is your favorite season? Why?

➢ Do you have a season that "weighs you down"? Which one and why?

➢ Is there a season that is more productive for you than another? Explain.

➢ Do you believe God has something planned for you?

➢ As you grow older, do you feel a sense of urgency to do what God has planned for you?

Challenge Yourself

❖ Make a list of qualities in each season.

❖ Try to make every moment count.

❖ Find a daily quiet time to listen to God's plan for you.

❖ ADD YOUR OWN CHALLENGE

April

April—Week 1

Philippians 3:21

NRSA
He will transform the body of our humiliation that it may be conformed to the body of his glory, by the power that also enables him to make all things subject to himself.

KJV
Who shall change our vile body that it may be fashioned like unto his glorious body, according to the working whereby he is able even to subdue all things unto himself.

"The Promise of Change"

Spring in Indiana is a mix of weather. It can be snowing one day and sunny and warm the next. The fluctuation from cold to warm continues throughout the following months, reminding us that the climate is as unpredictable as life.

Even with all that erratic weather lays assuredness of Spring—the promise of rejuvenation. Birds begin to sing and build nests. Grass slowly turns from a nasty brownish color to lush, cheery green. Flowers push their way through the ground and bloom. Our landscape is reborn.

One Spring, the lilies planted along the side of our home put on quite a show! They pushed their way through one of the coldest, snowiest winters to prove that nothing can stop them from revealing their beauty. I've heard people tell me that lilies are weeds. I'm glad that the lilies don't seem to think so. Otherwise, I don't think they would work so hard to blossom.

Those lilies remind us that the Easter season is coming. It, too, is filled with change and strength. Jesus walks through death to life, bringing us to life with Him. Spring is an opportunity to shake off the bleak, gray in our lives and to flourish. We can grow from what some may call a *weed* into a budding flower in God's garden. We can prove that Jesus can raise us above the trials we face and, as it's been said, "Bloom where you are planted"!

Points to Ponder

➤ How can we change the way we view *weeds* in our lives?

➤ Have you experienced a transformation in your life? Describe what happened.

➤ In what other ways do we witness change?

➤ Have you ever seen someone or something as being bad and then changed your mind? Explain.

➤ What helps you to shake off gray and flourish?

Challenge Yourself

❖ Take time to plant something.

❖ Make a conscious effort to look for a transformation in someone's life and your own.

❖ Pray for people you have viewed as *weeds*.

❖ ADD YOUR OWN CHALLENGE

April—Week 2

Leviticus 16:30

NRSA
For on this day atonement shall be made for you, to cleanse you; from all your sins you shall be clean before the Lord.

KJV
For on that day shall the priest make an atonement for you, to cleanse you, that ye may be clean from all your sins before the Lord.

"Spring Clean"

Usually, Spring is not considered the *crisp* season. That title belongs to Fall, but recently, while taking an early morning walk, *crisp* seemed to fit. It had been raining hard for the past two days so I was excited to get outside. As I bundled up in a warm jacket and even fastened my hood, I thought about the brisk air. Taking a deep breath, I thought how clean the air felt.

On that early morning hike, I met a neighbor walking his dog. Through his white beard he smiled brightly and exclaimed, "Good morning! Don't you just love this weather?!"

Smiling back, I stated, "It's the best—so crisp and clean!"

"Yes! That's it! It's clean! I hadn't thought of that but, yes, clean is the word," he cheerfully responded. All the way home, I thanked God for His gift of the Spring season and chance encounters.

Spring showers cleanse the earth so why can't those showers cleanse our lives? Our showers are the hope that we can bloom again just as the daffodils blossom into their bright, fresh yellow attire after the rain. As author Sarah Ban Breathnach said, "Expect to have hope rekindled. Expect your prayers to be answered in wondrous ways. The dry seasons in life do not last. The spring rains will come again."

Points to Ponder

➢ How does the season of Spring affect you?

➢ What is the difference between the terms, *crisp* and *clean*?

➢ Do you agree with Sarah Ban Breathnach's quote? Explain.

➢ Spring showers baptize the earth. Have you been baptized? Do you recall that experience? Why or why not is being baptized important?

Challenge Yourself

❖ Copy Sarah Ban Breathnach's quote and post it so you can reread it.

❖ Take a few minutes to *shower* yourself with good memories.

❖ ADD YOUR OWN CHALLENGE

Judges 18:10

NRSA

When you go, you will come to an unsuspecting people. The land is broad—God has indeed given it into your hands—a place where there is no lack of anything on earth.

KJV

When you go, you will come to an unsuspecting people. The land is broad—God has indeed given it into your hands—a place where there is no lack of anything on earth.

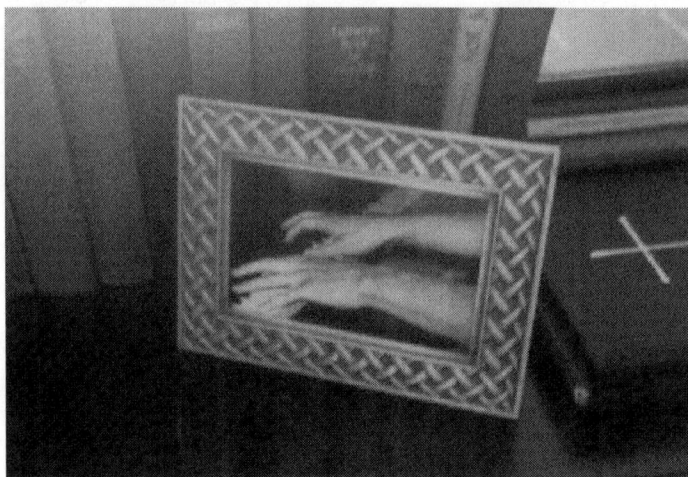

"The Touch of Hands"

Have you ever really looked at someone's hands? Hands tell so much about a person. The size, shape, and feel of the hands are significant. Their touch, however, reveals the inner spirit.

My husband has rough, thick hands with jagged cuticles because he bites them. They are often stained from a recent outdoor project or callused and scarred from manual labor. The look of his hands is that of a man who works hard at whatever he does.

There is a Danish proverb that says: "Who takes the child by the hand takes the mother by the heart." I love to look at the hands of my grandchildren. Each is unique—from the boxy-shaped thick fingers of one to the slender and freshly polished, and often peeled-off polish, of another. When I see them, I know their hands aren't completely finished. Years and activity will change the look of them.

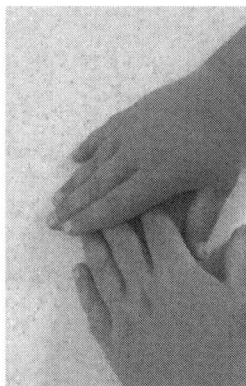

When I see a photo of hands, I can't help but think of my son, Zachary. He had long, thin fingers, chapped knuckles, and, like his father, chewed cuticles, but those fingers could make the piano keys dance. His hand was the last part of him I was able to see—the hand of a most remarkable young man with a magical touch.

One of Zachary's college roommates asked for a photo of Zachary's hands for his newly refurbished baby grand piano. I can think of no better way to honor Zack. He always wanted a baby grand and oh, how he loved to play the piano! What a marvelous tribute! His friend wanted to remember those hands.

Hands can be so many things: welcoming, admonishing, loving, and even clenching into a fist. Hands can create magic moments to fill our hearts and heads. Hands leave you remembering a certain touch.

Allow your hands to give gentle warmth, calm and reassuring love—a touch that will last a lifetime. Martin Luther King Jr. once said, "I have held many things in my hands, and I have lost them all; but whatever I have placed in God's hands that I still possess." All that we are remains in The Lord's hands.

Points to Ponder

➤ Do you use your hands a lot? How so?

➤ I had a friend to ask me why my hands were so scaly. I attributed the look of my hands to my age; however, I then decided I may not be taking care of them. How do you take care of your hands?

➤ In some cultures, using your hands certain ways may violate their beliefs. Can you describe such a culture?

➤ As you walk through life, pay special attention to how you use your hands:

     ○ Do you use your hands to welcome someone?

     ○ Do you admonish with your hands?

     ○ Do you show love with your hands?

Challenge Yourself
❖ Re-read the scripture. Reflect on it.
❖ Offer a helping hand to others.
❖ Take care of your hands—they are your tools.
❖ ADD YOUR OWN CHALLENGE

---

2 Corinthians 2:15

NRSA
For we are the aroma of Christ to God among those who are being saved and among those who are perishing.

KJV
For we are unto God a sweet savour of Christ, in them that are saved, and in them that perish.

"Hamburger Happiness"

When I was a little girl, my mom took my sister and I shopping downtown. I may be dating myself—but there were no malls. If you wanted to shop, downtown was the only option. I actually loved it!

After carrying our purchases inside and outside and store to store, the highlight of the day came when it was time to take a break for lunch. The smell of onions frying on a grill beckoned us to Hill's Snappy Service™, a few blocks away. I couldn't wait to get to that hamburger shop!

One day, my husband and I journeyed to the heart of Madison, a small town in southern Indiana. We walked the streets for a while before the familiar scent of grilled onions wafted in the air. Triggered by that recognizable aroma, the memory of that hamburger shop came rushing back. Once again, I was that little girl being drawn into the shop. Hinkle's Sandwich Shop™ has a long wooden bar and red

vinyl swivel stools with little else in the tiny café. The bar is lined with silver napkin dispensers, ketchup squeeze bottles, clear glass sugar cylinders and salt and pepper shakers. We quickly found two empty stools as my mind kept going back in time.

Munching on those delicious hamburgers, I was thankful for the ability to travel—both in the state of Indiana and in my mind. Joyfully lost in those feelings, I know God has given us these chances to smile and breathe in happiness—it's as simple as enjoying a hamburger.

Points to Ponder

➢ Do certain smells trigger memories for you?

➢ Has there been a place in your past that brings back a happy thought?

➢ What does the word *aroma* mean to you?

➢ If God gave you a scent, what would it be and why?

➢ What scents might you find in Heaven?

Challenge Yourself

❖ Next time you smell something you enjoy, savor that scent.

❖ Try to revisit a place from your past and/or record a memory.

❖ ADD YOUR OWN CHALLENGE

May

Deuteronomy 6:7

NRSA
Recite them to your children and talk about them when you are at home and when you are away, when you lie down and when you rise.

KJV
And thou shalt teach them diligently unto thy children, and shalt talk of them when thou sittest in thine house, and when thou walkest by the way, and when thou liest down, and when thou risest up.

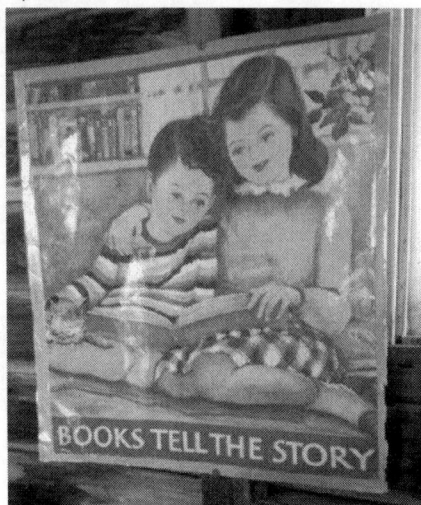

BOOKS TELL THE STORY

"Books Aplenty, Books Galore"

When I was little, my mom opened a new adventure to me each time she read. I'd see the heroes and villains, the setting and the action—all of the words created images only I could see. I remember begging her to read on so the story could keep floating in my head. Books give you the ability to form your own tales that can't be duplicated by anyone else.

After my mom retired, she gave me many of her books, but some of them weren't age appropriate for my kindergarten classroom. She and Dad stored those in the basement of his office. While cleaning out Dad's office, the books resurfaced. The boxes of books were from every genre. Most of the books were old but still useful. Books never go out of style!

Along with these books was a poster Mom hung in her classroom each year. Its caption read, "Books Tell The Story." I could envision that old poster above her classroom library. I thought about the influence the poster's words had on each student as they sifted through the books. Dr. Seuss once said, "You're never too old, too wacky, too wild, to pick up a book and read to a child."

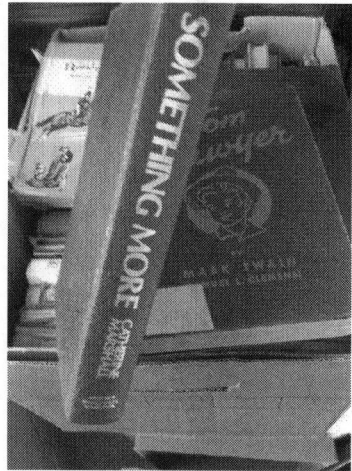

We have all been inspired by books. I recall Mom reading children's Bible books to me before I was even old enough for school. Today, I still go to that source of strength and wisdom.

Hopefully, you don't have to dust off your Bible to read about its adventures, its heroes and villains, and its life lessons. All of those can mold your life. Let the greatest book ever written open a door for you.

Points to Ponder

➤ Do you enjoy reading? What kind of literature do you read?

➤ Would Jesus approve of your reading material?

➤ What stories do you/did you read to your children?

➤ What is your first recollection of a Bible story?

➤ Which Bible stories have left an impact on your life? At what age do you recall reading or hearing that particular story?

➤ How often do you read the Bible?

Challenge Yourself

❖ Before reading something, ask yourself if you would recommend it to Jesus.

❖ As the scripture says, teach your children. Read to your children often.

❖ ADD YOUR OWN CHALLENGE

May—Week 2

Ephesians 4:16

NRSA
... from whom the whole body, joined and knit together by every ligament with which it is equipped, as each part is working properly, promotes the body's growth in building itself up in love.

KJV
From whom the whole body fitly joined together and compacted by that which every joint supplieth, according to the effectual working in the measure of every part, maketh increase of the body unto the edifying of itself in love.

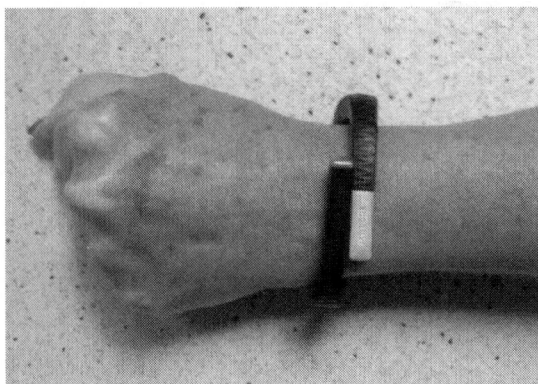

"In Sync"

Trying to keep in step with modern technology, I purchased a device called an UP by Jawbone™. I wear it on my wrist to track my physical activity. I download the information at the end of each day to my iPhone™ to see how many steps I've taken. I wish I could say that I bought the tracker because I wanted to improve my wellbeing, but that wouldn't be true. My husband, Dan and I need to document our exercising in order to qualify for better rates with our insurance company. We have always remained active but I must admit keeping a daily report of our activity has held us more accountable.

The first evening when I connected the Jawbone™ to my iPhone™, the words, "sync summary" appeared. The health sensor logged my daily movements. I thought, "Wow! Technology has made a lot of *strides* (pardon the pun)." All of a sudden, that phrase caused me to think about what it means to be "in sync".

I decided to look up the words. The definition of "in sync" is "working well together". The Jawbone™ worked well with my body to tally my steps for the day: working "in sync." The words hung as if in mid-air: **in sync**. Am I "in sync" in other areas of my life? Am I "in sync" with my family? How well does my mind work with my spirit? Am I "in sync" with God? I found myself doing a lot of self-reflection at that particular moment.

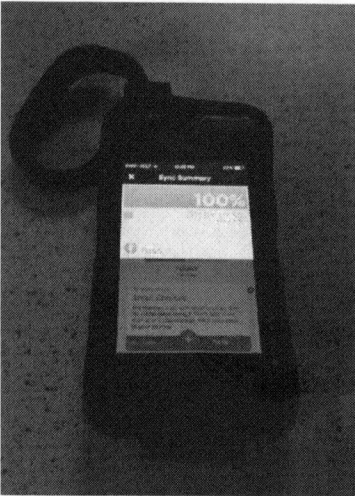

It's too bad that we don't have a device that records automatically when we pray or read our Bible. Perhaps it would hold us more accountable. I guess we have to do that the old fashioned way and write it down or perhaps program it into whatever new technology we have on hand. Our daily goal should be moving closer to our Lord—to be "in sync".

Points to Ponder

➤ What is your first memory of some new piece of technology in your life?

➤ Discuss how technology affects your life. Do you find it distracting or frustrating?

➤ How has technology helped you in your spiritual life?

➤ How are you "in sync" with God?

➤ What do you do to help you feel more connected with The Lord?

Challenge Yourself

❖ Work to be "in sync" with God.

❖ Make a list of new ways to build your spiritual life.

❖ ADD YOUR OWN CHALLENGE

Deuteronomy 30:13

NRSA
Neither is it beyond the sea, that you should say, "Who will cross to the other side of the sea for us, and get it for us so that we may hear it and observe it?"

KJV
Neither is it beyond the sea, that thou shouldest say, Who shall go over the sea for us, and bring it unto us, that we may hear it, and do it?

"An Ocean View"

The ocean has always been one of my favorite places on Earth. The sound of the waves lapping the shore, the fresh smell of the salt water, the sand between my toes, and the warmth of the sun lift my spirit. Just being there can brighten my day.

"People watching" is also an activity I enjoy. Walking along the beach, I overheard a woman ask a couple of young men, who were tossing a football to each other, if they would help her. Her son, who looked to be about the same age as the young men, was handicapped. The mother told these young men how her son longed to feel the ocean. Without hesitation, these two healthy teens moved to either side of her son. He put his arms around their shoulders and they walked him into the ocean so he could *feel* the waves. I stood and watched God's handiwork through them. The selfless act of helping another less fortunate was refreshing to my soul.

The next day, I again watched kindness flow through others. Three teenage girls helped a friend who was crippled. They made a cradle with their arms and the girl rested safely in their grasp. It was so exciting to watch the girls giggle together as the waves moved them back and forth. The ocean seemed to have healing power or at the very least, a lifting of their spirits.

The power of the ocean felt unlimited. It encompassed all of my senses. It seemed like God's spirit had reached out and brought out the best in everything and everybody as they helped each other *feel* the wonder of the ocean. We need to find that power each and every day!

Points to Ponder

➢ Where is your favorite place? Why is it your favorite?

➢ The people I saw longed to feel the waves. Why do you think they wanted to do this?

➢ Re-read the scripture. How does it apply to your life?

➢ Detail an act of kindness you have witnessed.

➢ In that act of kindness, were you able to see God's spirit at work? How could you tell?

Challenge Yourself

❖ Find a favorite place in God's creation.

❖ Look for an opportunity to do an act of kindness for another.

❖ Look for God in other acts of kindness you have witnessed.

❖ ADD YOUR OWN CHALLENGE

May—Week 4

Song of Solomon 2:12

NRSA
The flowers appear on the earth; the time of singing has come, and the voice of the turtledove is heard in our land.

KJV
The flowers appear on the earth; the time of the singing of birds is come, and the voice of the turtle is heard in our land;

"Turn Toward the Light and Bloom"

While walking down a cement path in Florida, along a row of green bushes, I spotted a solitary flower. It wasn't just a plain flower, but a bright, reddish-orange tropical one, blooming all alone. No other flower was in sight! How could this be?

As I continued my journey, the flower wouldn't leave my mind. I walked back to that flower and examined it closely. Reaching over the bright white railing, I sniffed the blossom. No scent. Still, this flower had made an impression on me. It made me smile to think about its determination to bloom when no other on the bush decided to do so. Although flowers don't really have personalities, this one seemed to take on a life of its own.

90

As I am not one who identifies flowers on sight, I researched it. I was excited to discover it was a Hibiscus. I found that this flower has lots of uses. In the Philippines, it is used by children as part of a bubble-making pastime. The hibiscus flower is traditionally worn by Tahitian and Hawaiian girls and is also Hawaii's state flower. Tea can be made of hibiscus flowers and is served both hot and cold. It even has health benefits such as lowering blood pressure. It is amazing what one flower is capable of producing!

How much are we like this flower? Comedian Jim Carrey said, "Flowers don't worry about how they're going to bloom. They just open up and turn toward the light and that makes them beautiful." Regardless of what is happening around us, we each can make the world a better place; we just need to turn toward the heavenly light and bloom.

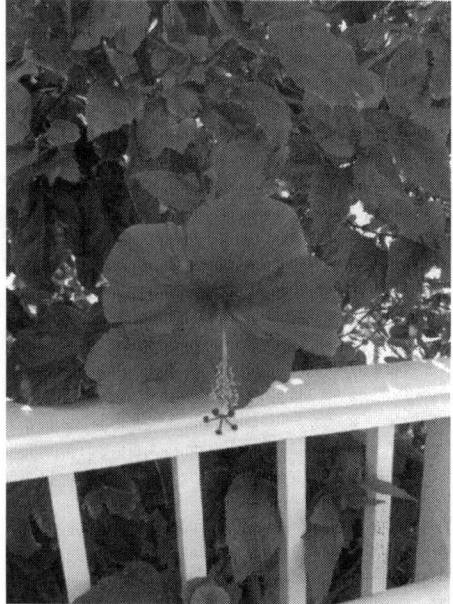

Points to Ponder

➤ What is your favorite flower and what makes it special for you?

➤ Compare yourself to a flower. What would you be?

➤ When have you felt as if you were trying to bloom alone?

➤ Do you find it easier to bloom alone or when you are surrounded by other Christians?

➤ In what ways are you useful?

Challenge Yourself

❖ Thank those who have helped you bloom.

❖ Take time to smell the roses or other fragrant flowers and things that give off a scent.

❖ ADD YOUR OWN CHALLENGE

June

2 Corinthians 8:13

NRSA
I do not mean that there should be relief for others and pressure on you, but it is a question of a fair balance between.

KJV
For I mean not that other men be eased, and ye burdened.

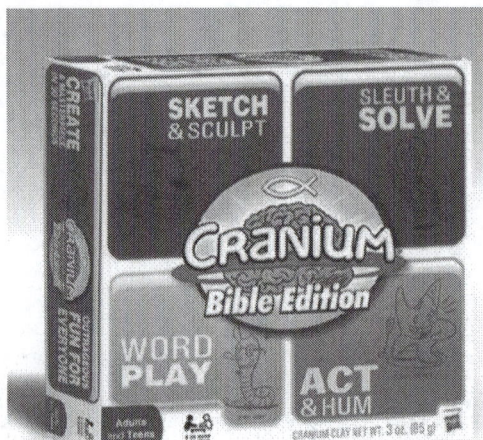

"Finding My Inner Balance"

Have you ever done something that you regretted right after you have done it? One evening, while playing the game Cranium™ with my children and their spouses, I drew the charades card for *The Karate Kid*. The first idea for the charade that popped into my head was the famous crane kick from the movie. Striking the pose, then with less than great poetic motion, I executed two sharp kicks.

My teammates promptly guessed the movie thanks to those kicks. I returned to my seat on the floor beside my husband, Dan. He gave me a quick punch on the forearm and asked, "How old do you really think you are?"

"What do you mean?" I responded. "I did the kicks, but my knee does kind of hurt." The knee continued to throb that night and the next day, but I assumed the pain would eventually go away.

After a month including several weeks of trying to work through the pain on my elliptical machine, I relented and saw a knee specialist. He pushed down on my knee, which about sent me through the examining table. The doctor told me he was certain the meniscus was torn, and promptly ordered an MRI (which is exactly what my son, Joel, the physical therapist, had told me the day after I injured it. Don't you just hate it when your kids are smarter than you?!)

Thinking of the lessons about the crazy kick made me focus on a response from the movie: Mr. Miyagi said, "Lesson not just karate only. Lesson for whole life. Whole life have a balance. Everything be better. Understand?"

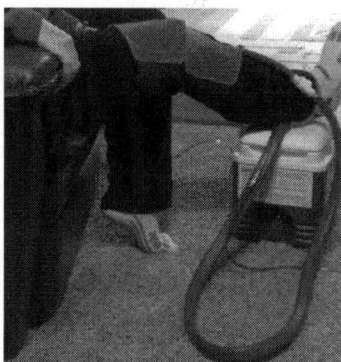

Thinking about that, I know that our Lord wants us to balance our lives. It must possess a steadiness—both physically and spiritually. In this busy world, it's how we choose to take obstacles and find the useful symmetry to once again make ourselves whole. Hopefully, the result of this injury will prove to be another way to "kick-start" the next life lesson for me and allow me to obtain a balance without regrets.

Points to Ponder

➢ Does your life seem out of balance? Why do you believe that happened?

➢ What did you do to get your life back on an even keel?

➢ Describe at least one event that taught you a lesson.

➢ Have you ever had to "kick-start" your life? How did you do it?

➢ Have you ever been a caretaker and by doing so, were you overwhelmed? Reveal your advice to others how to maintain a balance in your life.

Challenge Yourself

❖ Learn from your mistakes.

❖ If you are needed to help others, make certain to turn to Jesus for guidance to maintain your own life's symmetry.

❖ ADD YOUR OWN CHALLENGE

---

1 Corinthians 10:13

NRSA
No testing has overtaken you that is not common to everyone. God is faithful, and he will not let you be tested beyond your strength, but with the testing he will also provide the way out so that you may be able to endure it.

KJV
There hath no temptation taken you but such as is common to man: but God is faithful, who will not suffer you to be tempted above that ye are able; but will with the temptation also make a way to escape, that ye may be able to bear it.

"Sometimes Life is Full of Pooh"

Sometimes life just doesn't seem quite right. It feels...well, full of poo. Friends help shovel a path for us to see our way clear. I've always loved the stories of Winnie-the-Pooh and respected the pieces of wisdom from author, A.A. Milne.

> "We'll be friends forever, won't we,
> Pooh?" asked Piglet.
>
> "Even longer," Pooh answered.

I have needed friends more than ever, it seems. My parents are what some would call "snowbirds". They spend the winters in Florida and the other seasons back home in Indiana. As they have aged, they both lack in the hearing department and have other requirements that need to be addressed. Those of us who are fortunate enough to still have our parents with us, can rejoice at their smiles and laughter, and cry with their pain—and are confused as to know what to do to lend a hand especially when help is not requested but often necessary.

My friends have been such a blessing as I continue through this uncharted territory. They have called, sent messages, phoned to check on them, visited them, and even helped me pick them up at the airport. My friends have been there for me without my requesting but rather simply offering a

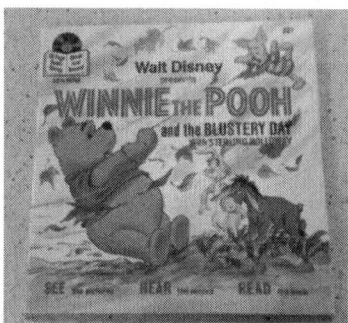

hand. Winnie-the-Pooh said, "You can't stay in your corner of the Forest waiting for others to come to you. You have to go to them sometimes." A.A. Milne was right, as my friends did just that: they came through my forest and helped.

Walking through the unknown, God will guide the way but friends help carry the equipment. I join with Pooh in saying, "When you see someone putting on his *Big Boots*, you can be pretty sure that an *Adventure* is going to happen."

Thanks, friends, for putting on your boots and backpack full of prayers to join me. My life is embarking on a unique adventure...full of Pooh and friends. Wisdom lies within children's books and through the eyes of a child.

> Piglet sidled up to Pooh from behind. "Pooh?" he whispered.
>
> "Yes, Piglet?"
>
> "Nothing," said Piglet, taking Pooh's hand. "I just wanted to be sure of you."

Thanks, friends, for letting me be sure of you.

101

Points to Ponder

➤ List some uncharted areas in your life.

➤ Do you believe that God will not let you be tested beyond your limits?

➤ Which Winnie-the-Pooh character is the most like you? What traits does that character have in common with you?

➤ Do you seek out friends or God's help first?

➤ Think of a recent test in your life. Explain how God has been there for you.

Challenge Yourself

❖ Give a friend a call or write them a note to thank them for supporting you.

❖ Write a note to God thanking Him for always being there for you.

❖ ADD YOUR OWN CHALLENGE

Acts 2:17

NRSA
In the last days it will be, God declares that I will pour out my Spirit upon all flesh, and your sons and your daughters shall prophesy, and your young men shall see visions, and your old men shall dream dreams.

KJV
And it shall come to pass in the last days, saith God, I will pour out of my Spirit upon all flesh: and your sons and your daughters shall prophesy, and your young men shall see visions, and your old men shall dream dreams.

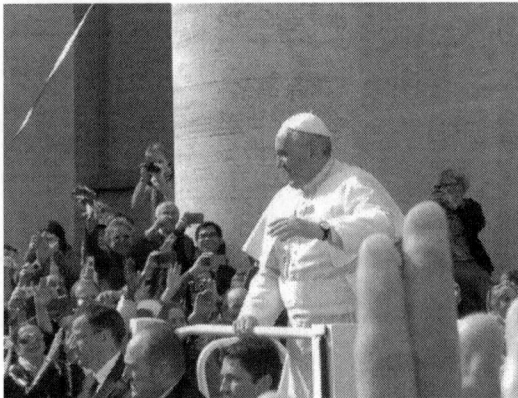

"Seeing the Pope"

It has been a dream of my husband's to see the Pope. Not having been raised Catholic; I wasn't really sure how I would feel when this event became a reality. It was truly a memory that will remain with me the rest of my life.

The crowd was so vast that it filled every nook and cranny of St. Peter's Square and spilled into the streets going beyond where the eye could see. We waited for hours and yet the time seemed to go by quickly. We were surrounded by persons from an assortment of nations speaking various languages. Those in front and behind us spoke Italian. Love transcended our language barriers. A smile, simple gestures and sharing of food needed no translation.

As the time of the Pope's arrival drew closer, cheers from the crowd grew to a roar. Excitement filled the air and swept us all away. Then, as those around us chanted, "Papa Francesco" or "Mia Papa," the Pope appeared! Being short in stature, a friend helped me climb onto a chair to get a closer look. Then, I saw him—not more than a few feet away! His face reflected love, kindness, and peace. You could actually feel the warmth of his love—Jesus shined through his eyes!

The feelings of being immersed in God's love brought tears to my eyes. As I climbed down from the chair, I looked into the eyes of an older Italian man. He, too, was wiping his tears. With his hand, the man motioned, touching his heart. I made the same gesture. Again, love knows no barrier.

When Pope Francis spoke, those thousands upon thousands of people stopped yelling and cheering. The entire audience grew still as night. The silence seemed as loud as the roaring crowd. It was Father's Day in Rome. Pope Francis quoted the Bible, imploring us all to help our children to grow, "in wisdom, age, and grace" (Luke 2:52). He invited us to rediscover our faith and to grow in charity.

This event has left an indelible mark in my life. As we grow older, may we live by example, become a reflection of Jesus' love and rediscover faith, hope and the greatest of these—love.

Points to Ponder

➢ Describe the dreams you have.

➢ Have your dreams become a reality? What did you do to make your dreams come to pass?

➢ Describe your feelings when you see someone who reflects Jesus.

➢ What are your thoughts about barriers between people? Have you experienced obstacles that have prevented you from communicating with someone?

➢ What event(s) have left a lasting memory? Can you recall your favorite part of that event?

Challenge Yourself

❖ Dare to dream. Re-evaluate your dream to make certain it is truly what you have dreamt of.

❖ Do everything in your own power to accomplish that vision.

❖ Work to break down obstacles.

❖ ADD YOUR OWN CHALLENGE

Psalm 92:1-3

NRSA

1 It is good to give thanks to the Lord, to sing praises to your name, O Most High; 2 to declare your steadfast love in the morning, and your faithfulness by night, 3 to the music of the lute and the harp, to the melody of the lyre.

KJV

1 It is a good thing to give thanks unto the LORD, and to sing praises unto thy name, O most High: 2 To shew forth thy loving kindness in the morning, and thy faithfulness every night, 3 Upon an instrument of ten strings, and upon the psaltery; upon the harp with a solemn sound.

"Whoa-oh-oh...Listen to the Music"

The plug-in radio seems to be a thing of the past. Nowadays, everyone uses other means to play music.

After my sister, Debby and I acquired our parent's cottage, connecting with the outside world is limited. The cottage is in a remote area without *Internet* access and limited satellite connections. We spent time cleaning and reorganizing to make more room for family visits. Work seems more fun if music is playing. I remembered that Dad had a radio and went on a hunt to locate it. After finding his paint splattered, old radio in a closet, we were carried back in time to an era of our youth—a time when you had to ever-so-slowly turn a dial and try to land on a specific station. If you turned too fast, you missed the station and only static blared out. I raised the slender silver antenna and adjusted the side dial slowly just as I'd done in my youth, and presto—music!

Dad had also saved the radio's "Use and Care Guide." As I looked at the old pamphlet, I thought, "Wouldn't it be great if each of us came with a use and care guide?" Wait a minute...we do! We have the Bible that tells us how to live and care for each other. We are like that old radio that functions well if we slow down, search for the right station and stretch out our antennas. Our lives are always moving too fast. We need to turn away from all the static and noise blaring around us, use prayer to help adjust our dials, and listen for God's still, calm voice.

As Debby and I worked and sang along, I thanked God for that old radio and that Heavenly music that moves us along making our work load lighter.

Points to Ponder

➤ What kinds of music do you like, e.g. classical, jazz, rag time, rhythm and blues, light rock, gospel?

➤ What time of day are you able to slow down enough to *stretch out your antenna, turn away from the static and noise,* and *pray?*

➤ What verses in the Bible do you like to guide you in your daily living?

➤ Does music help you to work better? Explain.

➤ Describe a time when you sang to the Lord.

Challenge Yourself

❖ Praise the Lord through music.

❖ Use the Bible as your guide to life's decisions.

❖ ADD YOUR OWN CHALLENGE

July

Deuteronomy 32:7

NRSA
Remember the days of old, consider the years of many generations; ask your father, and he will show you; your elders, and they will tell you.

KJV
Remember the days of old, consider the years of many generations: ask thy father, and he will shew thee; thy elders, and they will tell thee.

"A View from the Rear View Window"

Did you ever feel like you were stepping back in time? One summer day, Dan and I went to French Lick, Indiana with some good friends who own a Model A. We were excited to attend The Model A Restorers Club National Meet. Our friends, Ralph and Rainelle, have a beautiful Model A with a spacious back seat and invited us along for the ride. The day was particularly hot—90 degrees—but it was surprisingly quite pleasant. The summer breeze was cooling. We rode in comfort and style as other Model A owners joined in the procession.

While rambling down the road, other drivers waved and honked. People came out of their homes to watch these classic cars go by. Children stopped playing, pointed, and waved to us. As we waved and smiled back at them, I felt a connected bond of happiness and joy. The sight of these old cars had improved attitudes.

Looking out from the back window, time seemed to rewind. I thought about my dad's first car. It, too, was a Model A, which my mom had affectionately named Bessie. I'd heard stories about Bessie throughout my childhood. Stories of my mom taking off her shoes before entering so the carpet would stay clean, keeping a blanket handy for those cold, winter trips, and double-dating to the drive-in with their high school friends. This ride must have been similar to my parents in their youth. Perhaps my mom once had a view like mine.

Arriving at our destination, I had a greater appreciation for Bessie and the Model A. The ride was fun, not-too-fast, and simply enjoyable—just as life should be. Time moves by so fast that if we don't slow down, we miss the moments that bring us joy. We need to pause to take in the scenery—offer a wave every now and then to strangers along the way. Stop and remember: good friends and peaceful rides never go out of style.

Points to Ponder

➢ If you could go back in time, what period of time would you like to experience?

➢ Re-read the scripture. Relate a story that a parent, grandparent, or elder, have shared.

➢ Are you able to slow down enough to take in the scenery and allow yourself to stop and remember? Why or why not?

➢ Remember the past: good friends and peaceful rides. Share that story.

Challenge Yourself

❖ Make every moment count.

❖ Think about what you have learned from your elders and all they enjoyed in life.

❖ Share the stories of your past.

❖ ADD YOUR OWN CHALLENGE

Numbers 36:6

NRSA

This is what the Lord commands concerning the daughters of Zelophehad, "Let them marry whom they think best; only it must be into a clan of their father's tribe that they are married.

KJV

This is the thing which the LORD doth command concerning the daughters of Zelophehad, saying, Let them marry to whom they think best; only to the family of the tribe of their father shall they marry.

"Marriage and Watching Reruns"

In July, my high school sweetheart, Dan and I celebrate our anniversary. We are not the same persons that we were all those years ago. Life has changed and so have we. The Lord has blessed us with wonderfully talented, smart, caring children who married persons with those same attributes;

now our grandchildren are exhibiting similar traits. We've experienced the best of times...and definitely, the worst of times. But we've done it together.

People have asked us, "What is your secret?" It's no secret, really. A happy marriage should have God at the center. People change, everything changes—only God will never change. It is very difficult to be in a good relationship without God at the heart and in your hearts. Dan and I pray for strength and guidance each day.

A wedding anniversary is the celebration of love, trust, partnership, tolerance and most of all, friendship. While all the cards, flowers, music, the bells and whistles—things that make us feel romantic—are wonderful, they're not what really matters. It is prayer, loving and sharing that connect us. Dan and I are friends—really, very good friends.

I once read a quote from journalist Mignon McLaughlin that said, "A successful marriage requires falling in love many times, always with the same person." I guess it's like watching reruns on television from a splendidly comfortable, familiar show. My husband, Dan and I have been blessed...we watch a lot of reruns.

Points to Ponder

➤ In your life, how do you celebrate your anniversaries?

➤ Are you and your spouse the same persons you were when you were first married? How have you changed?

➤ Which memories do you savor?

➤ Is God at the center of your relationship and life?

➤ What steps should you take to ensure that God is first and foremost?

➤ Within the scripture, what do you think it means to marry "...*only into the family of your father's tribe*"?

Challenge Yourself

❖ Pray together as a couple.

❖ "Rerun" memories. Reflect.

❖ Use the scriptures as your guide in your marriage and life.

❖ ADD YOUR OWN CHALLENGE

Job 11:9

NRSA
Its measure is longer than the earth, and broader than the sea.

KJV
The measure thereof is longer than the earth, and broader than the sea.

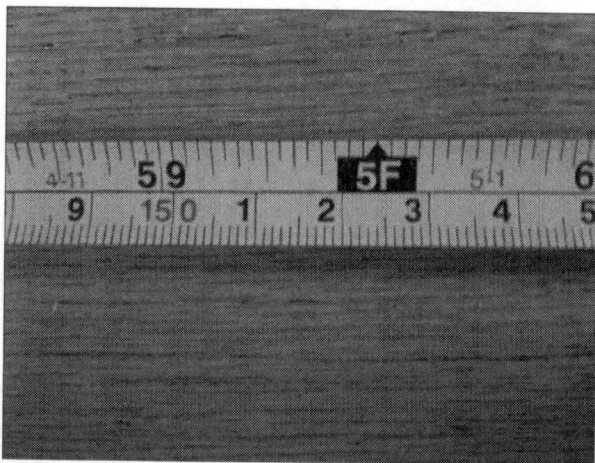

"Measuring Up"

Sixty marked a milestone birthday for me—and so it is with most people in the graduating class of 1973. I know that age is merely a number and shouldn't be the defining aspect of our lives, but it does give me pause to reflect on the events of my life. What have I done with these past 60 years? Were they worthwhile or do I need to reroute the path I'm on? What does the next day hold for me—or for the ones I love?

Once, I was shown my age by a tape measure. It was stretched out before me to demonstrate life. I looked closely at 60 inches, which by the way, is also my height. Looking at the numbers in front of me, it was clear it was longer at the start than the length remaining to reach 100 inches. I realized the numbers prior to 59 could not be changed, but the numbers in front are uncertain—with no guarantee of making it to 100.

A very dear friend and classmate spent her 60th birthday in the hospital. Her situation was sudden and unexpected. Despite the uncertainty of the situation, she worked to communicate with her children and express her love for them. Her inner strength stands as an example for all of us when confronted with dire circumstances.

The class of '73 rallied around her with prayers and encouraging words. We are not promised anything in life. The twists and turns along the way have not all been paved. Some of the roads are more than rocky but with the help of the Lord, family and good friends, the passage is a lot less bumpy.

I once read a birthday card that had a powerful message. It read, "As you grow up, make sure you have...more dreams than memories, more opportunities than chances, more hard work than luck and more friends than acquaintances. May you have the very best in life." As you look at your own life's tape measure, may the best years be stretched out in front of you.

Points to Ponder

➤ How does your life measure up?

➤ Describe something you've accomplished. How did that accomplishment make you feel?

➤ Would Jesus be proud of your accomplishment? Why or why not?

➤ As you look at the tape measure of your life, how would you describe your life thus far?

➤ Refer to a time when you rerouted your life. Describe it.

Challenge Yourself

❖ Make sure you have more dreams than memories.

❖ Make sure you have more opportunities than chances.

❖ Make sure you work toward a goal rather than leave life to chance.

❖ ADD YOUR OWN CHALLENGE

Deuteronomy 5:16

NRSA

Honor your father and your mother, as the Lord your God commanded you, so that your days may be long and that it may go well with you in the land that the Lord your God is giving you.

KJV

Honour thy father and thy mother, as the LORD thy God hath commanded thee; that thy days may be prolonged, and that it may go well with thee, in the land which the LORD thy God giveth thee.

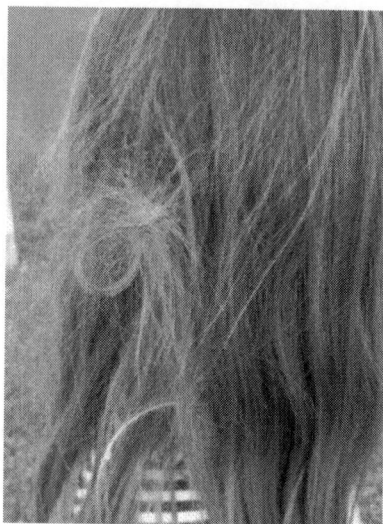

"Oh What a Tangled Mess"

Margo (known as "Nana" to our mutual grandchildren) and I were watching our grandson's baseball game. Our granddaughter Kendall came running over to us, pointed to a big tangle in her hair and said, "Before you get upset, this was an accident and it's all my fault."

We giggled a little and asked her to explain. She told us that her new friend was braiding her hair but Kendall had pulled out the rubber band. I rummaged through my purse for a comb or something to eliminate the tangle. Both grandmas worked on the situation but were unable to untangle the massive knot without resulting in a lot of, "Ouch! That hurts!" Finally, she dismissed our efforts, telling us, "It's alright. My mommy will fix it later. My new friend is waiting."

After the game, upon seeing the tangle, my son Joel said, "Kendall, what did you do?" As she retold the story, Joel whipped out his car key and began running the key through the knot. Yes, there was protesting, but only for a short while as her father worked on her hair. Kendall trusted that her dad knew what he was doing and the knot would be gone. Joel did just that—he took care of the mess.

Father's Day gave me time to reflect on the incident. Isn't that tangle just like life? Many people try to fix a problem, but it takes a strong father who, like God, takes care of a mess and straightens it out. I'm grateful to fathers who take charge of their children, letting them know that they are in good hands.

Points to Ponder

➤ Recount a time that you can remember your parent resolving a *tangled mess* for you.

➤ Have you, as a parent, resolved a *tangled mess* for your child? Describe it.

➤ Are you a *take charge* parent? Why or why not?

➤ Do your children rely on you? Is their reliance upon you an acceptable amount?

➤ Explain how you know that your children honor you as described in the scriptures.

Challenge Yourself

❖ Think before you act—resist being impulsive.

❖ Be sure that you always honor your father and mother as per the scriptures, no matter your age.

❖ Make certain that you expect that your children show you respect and honor.

❖ ADD YOUR OWN CHALLENGE

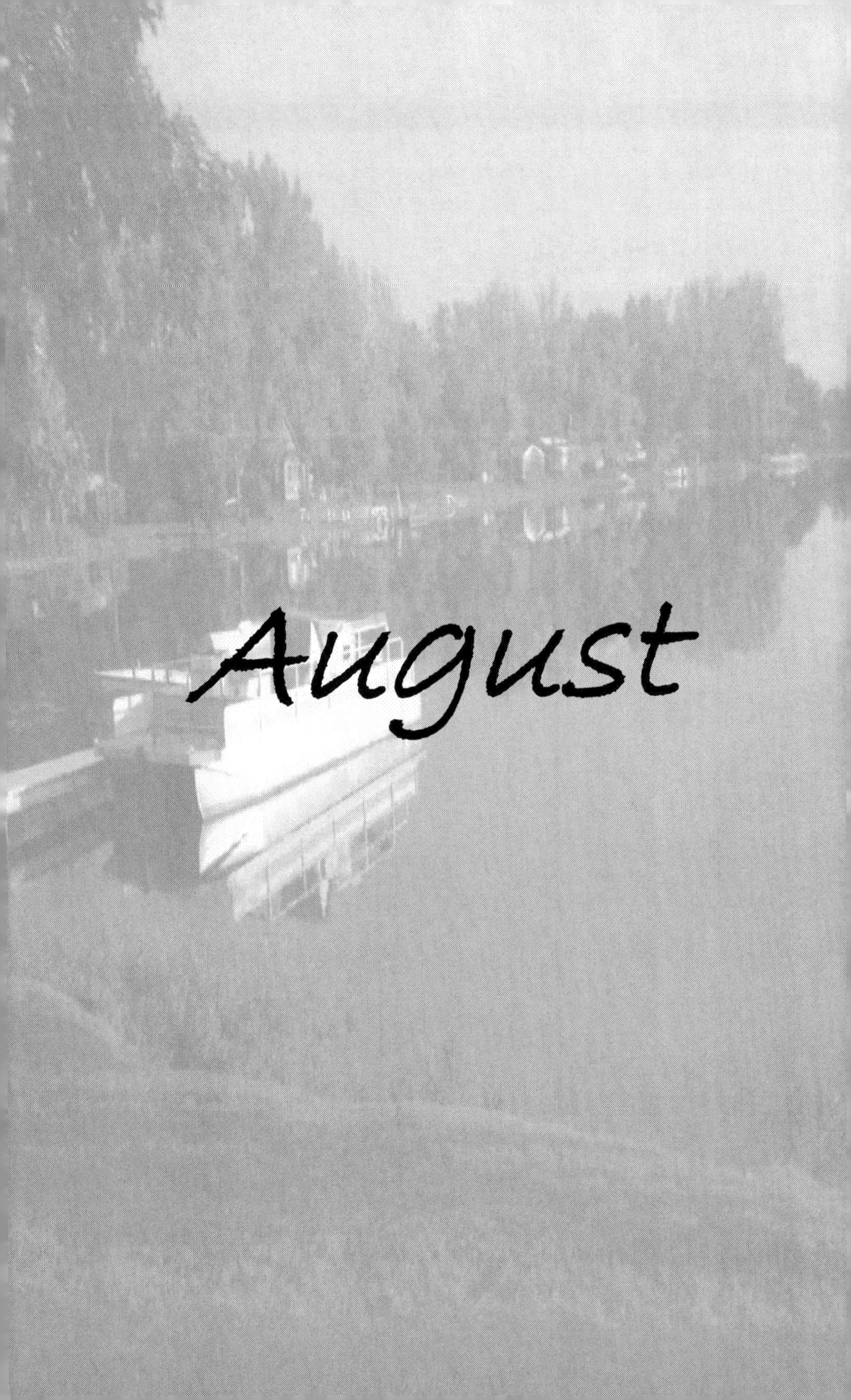

August

August—Week 1

Ecclesiastes 11:9-10

NRSA

⁹Rejoice, young man, while you are young, and let your heart cheer you in the days of your youth. Follow the inclination of your heart and the desire of your eyes, but know that for all these things God will bring you into judgment. ¹⁰ Banish anxiety from your mind, and put away pain from your body; for youth and the dawn of life are vanity.

KJV

⁹Rejoice, O young man, in thy youth; and let thy heart cheer thee in the days of thy youth, and walk in the ways of thine heart, and in the sight of thine eyes: but know thou, that for all these things God will bring thee into judgment. ¹⁰ Therefore remove sorrow from thy heart, and put away evil from thy flesh: for childhood and youth are vanity.

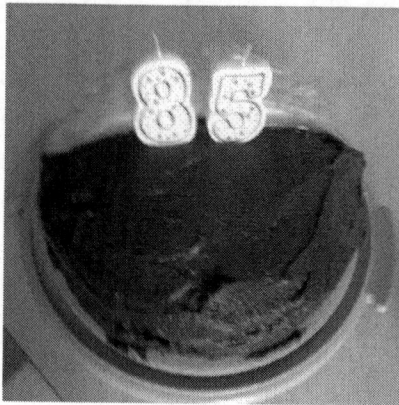

"Icing on the Cake"

Baking a cake for family birthdays is a standing tradition for me, but only if requested. Otherwise, a purchased cake will do. Usually, I make chocolate or vanilla and frost the cake with one flavor of icing—nothing fancy, but yummy all the same. One particular year, my mother-in-law requested a homemade cake for her 85th birthday. I had an idea: why not frost the cake with both flavors? Make it half and half so that the flavor accommodates everyone.

Each year is a new slice in our cake of life. Ann Landers once said, "At age 20, we worry about what others think of us. At age 40, we don't care what they think of us. At age 60, we discover they haven't been thinking of us at all." I do not think of old age as a time that I must endure, but as a time of adventure and freedom. No longer is my life centered on punching a time clock. The new slice of life has provided a taste to explore whatever I wish, chocolate or vanilla, and the time with friends and family, well—that's the icing on the cake.

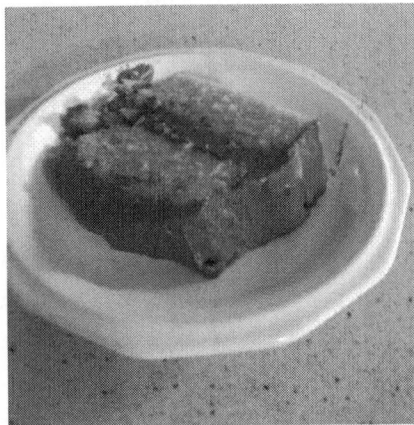

Birthdays mark the years and provide us with an element of excitement and surprise. No one can live forever, but you can make the best of your life. Enjoy it as much as possible, and give joy with each bite of a new day. Take a deep breath, blow out the candles and wish for the stars. You might just get them no matter what age!

Points to Ponder

➢ Re-read the scripture. Are you stuck in a rut in your life, doing the same things over and over again?

➢ How can you add variety to your life?

➢ Do you like birthdays? Why or why not?

➢ Is death something you fear? Explain.

➢ What flavor do you add to life?

➢ How do you think others perceive you—one who gives joy and appreciates life or one who gives off negative energy?

Challenge Yourself

❖ Change your daily activities by doing one new thing per day.

❖ Speak no evil—be positive when talking to others.

❖ Be the icing on someone's cake today.

❖ ADD YOUR OWN CHALLENGE

Genesis 1:20

NRSA

And God said, "Let the waters bring forth swarms of living creatures, and let birds fly above the earth across the dome of the sky."

KJV

And God said, Let the waters bring forth abundantly the moving creature that hath life, and fowl that may fly above the earth in the open firmament of heaven.

"Peaceful Waters"

Where do you go to find peace? When you shut your eyes and think of a spot that you could go and relax, where is it? For me, one place is water. Something about getting away from the hustle and bustle of the world by escaping to the water's edge calms my soul.

When I was a little girl, we rented a small cottage on Big Barbie Lake in northern Indiana. I would dangle my feet off the end of the pier and gaze across the water. The soft lapping of the cool water against my toes refreshed my mind. As my hair would blow in the soft breeze, it felt as if God was right there, all around me.

In the late seventies, our family shifted locations to another northern Indiana lake: Rock Lake. Looking at the evening sunset on the still, calm water, the childlike feelings resurface. God's love and peace sweep over me and I thank God for so many things in my life. We all need to find peace. Find a place and wait for Him.

Points to Ponder

➤ Close your eyes. Think of a place that you could go and relax. Where is it?

➤ Are you alone or with someone else at your peaceful place?

➤ Re-read the scripture. Do you go to your peaceful place to find God?

➤ Is nature part of that peace? Why or why not?

Challenge Yourself

❖ Eliminate the stresses of life in your peaceful place.

❖ Find a time and place to meet God.

❖ Share your peace with others.

❖ ADD YOUR OWN CHALLENGE

Proverbs 18:24

NRSA
Some friends play at friendship but a true friend sticks closer than one's nearest kin.

KJV
A man that hath friends must show himself friendly: and there is a friend that sticketh closer than a brother.

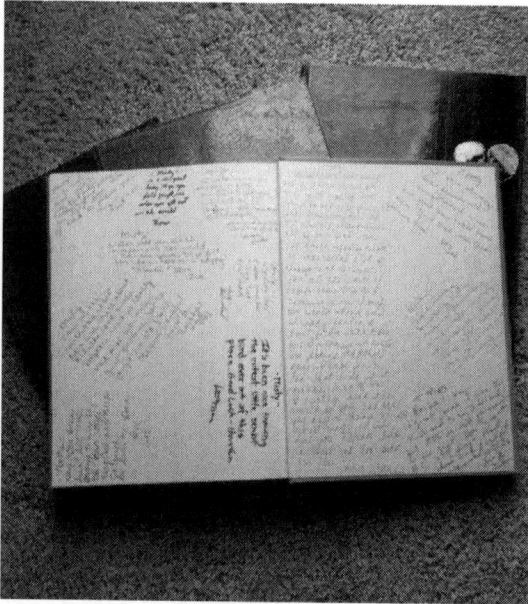

"Looking Back"

Looking through my closet one day, I stumbled upon my old high school yearbooks. Opening my senior book, I read those messages written by my classmates so many years ago. I've thought about what it would be like to go back through those school days. Would I do things differently?

Would I have had the same friends? Would my life be different?

Throughout the years, I have had the chance to see friends and acquaintances from my school days at reunions and chance encounters. At those times, looking into their faces, I see the eyes of the past. For a brief moment, I even feel younger.

Some time ago, I ran into an old high school friend. We were acquaintances in school but never really "hung out". We chatted for over an hour like we had been in touch for years. I was sorry that we hadn't really connected back then but was grateful for the chance to visit now.

Some good friends remain good friends. They "have my back," so to speak. We call one another when we need a listening ear, some honest advice or just talk. We pick up where we left off, whether it was just yesterday or months or even years since we last visited.

As this new school year begins, reflect on the friendships you made and the lessons you learned. We can't go back and relive our past, but we can choose to make a difference with the future. God has blessed me with friends, both new and old. Friendship isn't about whom you have known the longest. It's about who has your back and chooses to stay by your side.

Points to Ponder

➤ List at least 5 qualities you want in a friend.

➤ Reflect on your friendships. Are there differences between your friends?

➤ Consider those you call friends and explain why they are good friends.

➤ If you could go back through life, what things would you do differently in choosing your friends?

➤ Re-read the scripture. Are you a true friend?

Challenge Yourself

❖ Be a good listener.

❖ Be prepared to give honest advice.

❖ Be available to listen to someone in need.

❖ ADD YOUR OWN CHALLENGE

August—Week 4

James 1:6

NRSA
But when he asks, he must believe and not doubt, because he who doubts is like a wave of the sea, blown and tossed by the wind;

KJV
But ask in faith, never doubting, for the one who doubts is like a wave of the sea, driven and tossed by the wind;

"Life's Drawbridge"

When I was teaching kindergarten, I taught the kids a song about an imaginary castle on a hill with a drawbridge and a watch tower. It was such fun to sing about that imaginary castle. Who would have ever thought I'd encounter a drawbridge in real life?

While leaving my parents' condo in Florida, we were stopped by a crossing gate, much like that of a railroad crossing bar, where the road passed over an inner-coastal waterway. It had a guard station similar to the watch tower in the song. My sister and I watched in amazement as two large sections of road were drawn up into the air and a vessel from the ocean passed through the opening.

Jumping out of the stopped car, I began snapping pictures. The old song played in my head while watching the event

144

unfold. My vantage point did not allow me to get a good picture of the ship. The drawbridge action was an incredible sight to see!

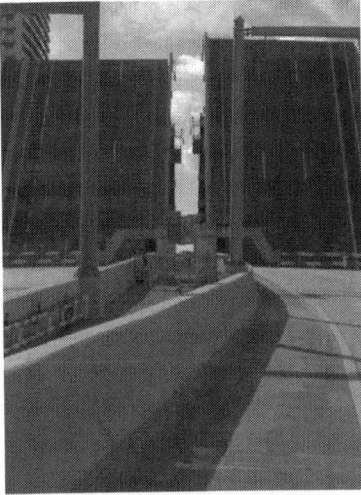

In our lives, each of us has our own personal, real drawbridge. We decide who we grant access into our lives. We allow some to come into our lives, while for others we pull up the bridge and let them simply pass through and move on. Having that control is a powerful tool.

If we allow the Bible to guide us, it tells who should stay and who should go. Chaos and insignificant drama are not allowed within God's castle. Permit entrance only to those who make us a better version of ourselves, those who follow God's way. When we take charge over our own drawbridge, we find passage into a Christ-centered life.

Points to Ponder

➤ Do you believe we each have our own drawbridge? Explain.

➤ Have you experienced persons in your life when you had to pull up your drawbridge?

➤ If so, was it difficult to let that person pass through your life?

➤ What does the guard house represent in your life and who is in that house?

➤ What do you think the scripture means? Have you ever doubted your faith?

Challenge Yourself

❖ Take time to reflect on your life and the people in it.

❖ Think about obstacles in your life and how you handled them. Did you exercise your faith?

❖ Use your drawbridge effectively.

❖ ADD YOUR OWN CHALLENGE

september

Isaiah 43:19

NRSA

I am about to do a new thing; now it springs forth, do you not perceive it? I will make a way in the wilderness and rivers in the desert.

KJV

Behold, I will do a new thing; now it shall spring forth; shall ye not know it? I will even make a way in the wilderness, and rivers in the desert.

"Taking a Drip"

Summer is slipping...and dripping away. How can this be? I recall starting school after Labor Day and ending for summer vacation after Memorial Day. Times change, but new lessons are always on the horizon, whether you are in or out of school.

Trips to the ice cream shop may slow down along with other summer activities, but I will choose to keep dipping into the delight beyond the season. I prefer hand-packed, hard ice cream, but occasionally, soft-serve dipped in chocolate is a great change of pace. Change can be a challenge. I am reluctant to try new flavors because venturing into unknown territory may result in disappointment. But new adventures can thaw the soul. Good things come in all sizes and flavors—and last year round.

Growing up, homemade ice cream was a rare and special treat. Dad would set up the ice cream maker on our back porch. The machine would grind and grind. More salt and ice needed to be added during the process. The work had to be monitored so that the ice cream turned out. We could hardly wait for that sweet, creamy treat! My husband, Dan, continues the tradition. It still takes just as long today as it did then—sometimes patience is worth the wait.

Choose your adventure. Investigate something new. Explore all options—whether at home or away. As the famous playwright, Thornton Wilder said, "My advice to you is not to inquire why or whither, but just to enjoy your ice cream while it's on your plate."

Raise your ice cream in remembrance of good times and new memories in the making. Make a toast to learning and new experiences. Take pleasure in each drip and savor each moment before it melts away.

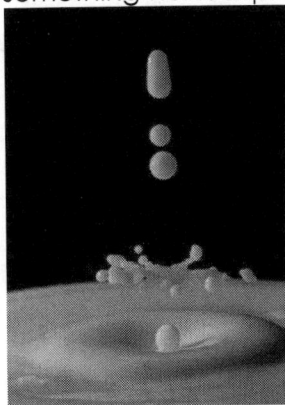

Points to Ponder

➤ What flavor of ice cream is most like your personality? Why?

➤ Re-read the scripture. Reflect on your life. How do you react to something new?

➤ Are there any changes coming up in your life?

➤ What sweet memories do you have of your past?

➤ Do you have the courage to choose a new adventure or investigate something new? Why or why not?

Challenge Yourself

❖ Don't get stuck in the past.

❖ Seek out a new adventure.

❖ Write about good changes in your life.

❖ ADD YOUR OWN CHALLENGE

---

1 Corinthians 4:10

NRSA
We are fools for the sake of Christ, but you are wise in Christ. We are weak, but you are strong. You are held in honor, but we in disrepute.

KJV
We are fools for Christ's sake, but ye are wise in Christ; we are weak, but ye are strong; ye are honourable, but we are despised.

"Applesauce"

Apples have long been associated with the biblical story of Adam and Eve, although there is actually no mention of the specific kind of fruit. Much like the unnamed fruit in the Bible, good or bad things can result from what we produce.

In our front yard, we have a once misunderstood apple tree. It has crazy apples—our misfits or rebels of the apple world whose shape and size defy the ordinary. These are the ones we see as different. They don't have the typical apple traits.

After peeling and coring these apples, my husband, Dan and I discovered that their insides are as good, if not better than the average apple. Their flavor is tart, but yet not too tart; making the perfect applesauce. I am glad we didn't push them aside or ignore them. While some may see them as the peculiar ones, if given a chance, we can see their value and unique worth.

These apples are much like us. No matter the shape, the outer skin or the size, the inner content is valuable and will, if given the chance, produce good work—or in this case, great sauce!

Points to Ponder

➢ Do you recognize qualities in yourself that make you a misfit? List those qualities.

➢ Do you see qualities in others that affect your like or dislike of those people? Why do they affect you?

➢ Can you ignore those qualities in yourself that you believe represent frailties and weaknesses?

➢ If you strive to be Christ-like, can you overlook those qualities in others that you *despise*? Why or why not?

➢ Re-read the scripture. In what ways can you hold yourself and others in a position of honor as Christ holds you in honor? Could you put that into practice in your daily life?

Challenge Yourself

❖ Refrain from being judgmental.

❖ Treat others as you want to be treated.

❖ Strive to be more like Christ.

❖ ADD YOUR OWN CHALLENGE

September—Week 3

James 1:12

NRSA

Blessed is anyone who endures temptation. Such a one has stood the test and will receive the crown of life that the Lord has promised to those who love him.

KJV

Blessed is the man that endureth temptation: for when he is tried, he shall receive the crown of life, which the Lord hath promised to them that love him.

"Wearing Many Hats"

While cleaning out my mother's closet, my sister Debby and I ran across some hat boxes. We were surprised when we opened the lids to find the hats in such good condition. Most of the hats were from past eras bringing a feeling of days gone by. Just looking at each one transported us to a memory from our childhood. Mom often wore hats to church or special events. I always thought they made her look regal.

We asked Mom about some of the hats and if she had a favorite. She didn't recall a favorite. She told us that she did enjoy wearing them and remembered wearing all of them but one. Debby and I found it odd that the navy and white hat we liked the most was the hat Mom simply didn't ever recall wearing.

I began to think about how many hats we all wear, metaphorically. We are often wearing many at the same time—child, sister, wife, mother, friend, and the list goes on and on—cook, housekeeper, dishwasher, nurse, teacher, etc. Finally my mind rested on the most important hat of all: Christian. Do I ever take off that hat?

As I put Mom's hats back onto the shelf, I said a prayer thanking God for each hat. They each have a special place in my life and I pray that when I am in the moment, whether it is scrubbing stains out of soiled laundry or enjoying time with my friends—my love of Christ is regally displayed.

Points to Ponder

➤ Make a list of all the different hats you wore as a child. Then list the hats you wear now. What's the difference? Which list is more Christ-like? Why do you think that is so?

➤ If you could only have three *hats*, what hats would you select?

➤ In what ways do you project Jesus in your everyday life? What could you do to become more like Jesus?

➤ Re-read the scripture. In what ways can you hold yourself and others in a position of honor as Christ holds you in honor? Could you put that into practice in your daily life?

Challenge Yourself

❖ Put on your 'crown' today.

❖ Look for others who project Christ-like qualities.

❖ Focus on wearing only the most important hats and write them down.

❖ ADD YOUR OWN CHALLENGE

Isaiah 46:10

NRSA
"...declaring the end from the beginning and from ancient times things not yet done, saying, "My purpose shall stand, and I will fulfill my intention,""

KJV
"Declaring the end from the beginning, and from ancient times the things that are not yet done, saying, My counsel shall stand, and I will do all my pleasure:..."

"The Iron Bridge"

While driving down a country road, there, along the side of the road, surrounded by weeds, was an old rusty, iron bridge crossing...well, crossing nothing. The weather and elements had corroded the towering steel beams. It stood out like a sore thumb. It felt strange that the bridge led to nowhere. It no longer served a useful purpose. Was the bridge once used to cross a ravine or a river? What was its history?

Staring at that bridge, I reflected on its existence. The bridge still had a powerful presence. Its imposing size interrupted the landscape, calling out to be noticed. The existence of this old relic along the side of the road illustrated the richness and strength of its past, while reflecting the passage of time.

Like the bridge, I too, have aged. Time has left its scars on me and occasionally, my body feels a bit rusty. I choose to push on and try to make a difference in the landscape of life. The famous playwright, Thornton Wilder once said, "There is a land of the living and a land of the dead and the bridge is love, the only survival, the only meaning."

Each of us has spent time standing out in what seems to be a lonely field. Pull those weeds that surround us. Turn weakness into strength and make a connection to someone in need of finding a purpose. Make the landscape both more useful and beautiful. God has given each of us a purpose. Strive to be a bridge of love that survives through the elements and stands the test of time.

Points to Ponder

➢ Have you ever felt as if you were on a road or path going nowhere? Did you have a plan or a direction for your life to take? Did you follow that plan? Why or why not?

➢ Re-read the scripture. Now that you have some life experiences, reflect. What would you have done differently in your life?

➢ Even now, on this very day, do you have a plan or a direction for your future? How is that plan different from the manner in which you have already lived your life?

➢ Do you have areas of weakness that need to be strengthened? Does your plan for your future strengthen those areas of weakness?

➢ Are you living according to God's purpose for you? How do you know?

Challenge Yourself

❖ Reflect upon your life. Seek to be strong.

❖ Be open to change in your life.

❖ Seek out God's purpose for your life.

❖ ADD YOUR OWN CHALLENGE

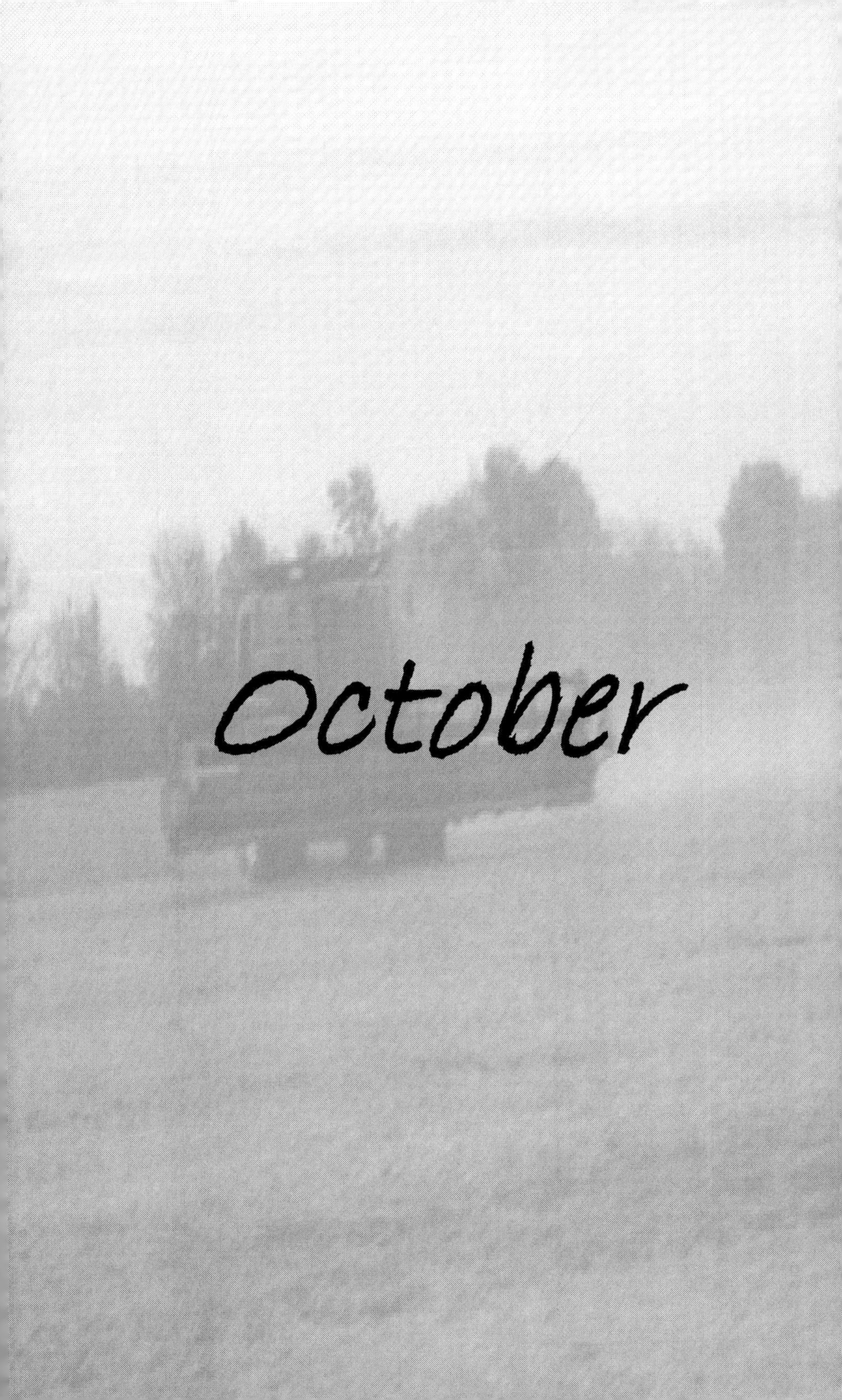

October

October—Week 1

Romans 12:3

NRSA
For by the grace given to me I say to everyone among you not to think of yourself more highly than you ought to think, but to think with sober judgment, each according to the measure of faith that God has assigned.

KJV
For I say, through the grace given unto me, to every man that is among you, not to think of himself more highly than he ought to think; but to think soberly, according as God hath dealt to every man the measure of faith.

"What's Your Mission?"

Mission Trip...whenever those words are heard, I envision a place far away; a place located somewhere requiring a passport, a plane ride to get to the destination and a week or more away from home.

I was blessed to go on a mission trip only hours from home in Springfield, Illinois. We packed a lot into three days. Even though I wasn't a member of the church sponsoring the trip; the group made me feel more than welcome.

Our primary purpose was to work at a distribution center that helps people in need inside and outside of our country. For example, kits containing cleaning supplies are sent to areas suffering adversity. The center also assembles kits for babies, makes desks out of scrap bleachers, fixes bicycles (literally hundreds of bikes), and repairs old sewing machines. It was amazing to see the vast number of items organized and ready to be sent at a moment's notice. Who would have thought a place needing our help was just a few hours away?

We also worked a bread line that serves more than 600 people a day. Some of our group washed dishes, others helped prepare food for future meals, and a couple of us served food. It was humbling to be a small part of such a big operation. It was a blessing to be able to greet each person and pray for them as they went through the line. I couldn't help but think, "There but for the grace of God, go I."

Now when I hear the words, Mission Trip, I won't form a vision of a place outside my reach. Our mission in life can start here and now. There are needs all around us. We can pray for the person in line at the grocery or the person in the car beside us.

The bottom line is missions aren't about us or our "projects"— they are about seeking God's purpose. Missions are about making a difference...and sometimes the mission trip is right where you are.

More information can be found at:
http://www.midwestmissiondc.org/

Points to Ponder

➢ Have you ever considered a mission trip? If so, where would you like to go and what would you like to do?

➢ What do you consider to be your mission?

➢ Re-read the scripture. Do you have areas in your community that need assistance? Where are they?

➢ If you don't have a home church, do you think you'll be able to make connections to be a part of a mission trip? How will you make connections or who will you contact?

➢ If you find a place to serve, in your community or elsewhere, do you believe you will follow through? Why or why not?

Challenge Yourself

❖ Strive to make a difference.

❖ Look around your community for wants and needs of others.

❖ Stretch yourself and commit to a mission trip.

❖ ADD YOUR OWN CHALLENGE

Deuteronomy 32:10

NRSA

He sustained him in a desert land, in a howling wilderness waste; he shielded him, cared for him, guarded him as the apple of his eye.

KJV

He found him in a desert land, and in the waste howling wilderness; he led him about, he instructed him, he kept him as the apple of his eye.

"The Apple Tree"

We have an apple tree in our front yard, and some years its fruit is exceptionally plentiful. One year, the tree was so full that it was struggling under the weight of the abundant crop. In hopes of supporting it, my husband, Dan placed a two by four under a nearly broken branch to act as a crutch.

During the month of October, the apple tree is a source of much activity. Our grandkids join us with the picking and cooking of the apples as well as making pies, applesauce and apple butter to share with family, friends and neighbors. Our home is continuously filled with the aroma of what I now think of as "the scent of fall."

I often look at our apple tree and see many connections to life. How many times do I not use the fruit or gifts God has given me or just plain misunderstand the purpose? And that *two by four crutch*—don't we all need to be held up every now and then—whether it is in the form of prayer or actual physical help? Aren't we all just finding where we fit into the "pie" God is creating? Sometimes the most obvious everyday things ground us and let us know that we are all "the apple of His eye."

Points to Ponder

➤ What do you consider to be your strengths?

➤ Do you believe your strengths are gifts from God? Why or why not?

➤ Where do you fit into God's *pie* to fulfill His purpose?

➤ Have you been called by God to help others? Did you act on that call? If not, why not?

➤ Re-read the scripture. Are you lost or has God instructed you a way to use your gifts he has given you for a greater purpose?

Challenge Yourself

❖ Consider praying for someone new each day.

❖ Make it a part of your daily living to help others.

❖ Strive to be *the apple of His* eye—to fulfill God's purpose for you.

❖ ADD YOUR OWN CHALLENGE

Exodus 23:16

NRSA

You shall observe the festival of harvest, of the first fruits of your labor, of what you sow in the field. You shall observe the festival of ingathering at the end of the year, when you gather in from the field the fruit of your labor.

KJV

And the feast of harvest, the first fruits of thy labours, which thou hast sown in the field: and the feast of ingathering, which is in the end of the year, when thou hast gathered in thy labours out of the field.

"Seasoning Sense"

Autumn is in the air! You can smell it on the breeze. What signals the change of seasons in Indiana? The temperature falls and the crops slow down. Every now and then, there is more than a hint that cold weather's coming.

My husband has been working hard preparing for the cold weather. The buzz of the chain saw, the pop of the log splitter followed by the smell of freshly chopped wood, alert the neighbors that the season is changing. We huddle around bonfires and move with each shift of the wind to avoid getting smoke in our eyes. That smoky scent lingers on your clothes long after the fire is out—all of the sounds and smells of the crisp, colorful season.

One of my best friends, Beth, married a farmer. I've heard of the hard work around the farm and the harvesting time that revolves around the weather. Sometimes her husband, Gordon is in the fields for days. Timing is crucial. Whenever I see farmers, I can't help but respect and appreciate their hard work.

The season of autumn is the transition from warm to cold weather. Even if we are not ready for the next season, it will happen. As we walk through life, we should get ready for the unexpected and harvest the fruits of our labor. Changing weather in our lives is inevitable yet unpredictable. It is up to us to store up His Word so we are ready when life gets cold. If prepared, we can huddle around the warmth of God's love and find the sweet scent of faith and hope that will remain long after the smoke has vanished.

Points to Ponder

➢ What comes to your mind when you think of autumn?

➢ Do you have memories of huddling around a camp fire in those autumn months? Describe those memories.

➢ Do you prepare for the upcoming season in some special way? Explain those preparations.

➢ Re-read the scripture. List the fruits of your labor.

➢ Why is reading God's word important to you?

Challenge Yourself

❖ Share the fruits of your labor.

❖ Prepare for the upcoming season.

❖ ADD YOUR OWN CHALLENGE

Romans 8:39

NRSA
...nor height, nor depth, nor anything else in all creation, will be able to separate us from the love of God in Christ Jesus our Lord.

KJV
Nor height, nor depth, nor any other creature, shall be able to separate us from the love of God, which is in Christ Jesus our Lord.

"Feeling Tall When You Are Small"

It's true that I am *not* nor have I ever been really too tall. Shoulders back and standing straight as possible, my stature remains all of five foot. I've not always been considered too small. In sixth grade, I was actually average to above average in height. But after sixth grade, my adult height was cast.

My husband Dan, my sister Debby, her husband Ervin, my nephew, David and I took a trip to the California Redwoods. Standing among (and inside) the tallest trees on Earth, I felt smaller than I've ever felt. I was like an ant as these ancient forest timbers towered above us. They seemed to swallow us whole! As we hiked among these trees, it felt as though I was walking through a fairy tale. These giants gave me pause to think about life before people were created. The Redwoods made me feel as if I were taking a prehistoric journey. Some of these trees have been around since the birth of Christ. Surely God made such majestic trees to enable us to catch a glimpse of the power and mystique of the world around us.

The Redwood survival strategies are diverse and complex. The fact is that these trees cannot attain their true size and stature without specific conditions to nurture them. The bark of a Redwood is very thick and demonstrates an unusual quality when exposed to fire—it scorches into a heat shield, similar to that of a space vehicle as it re-enters the Earth's atmosphere. Even though several of the trees were extremely burnt, they remained alive.

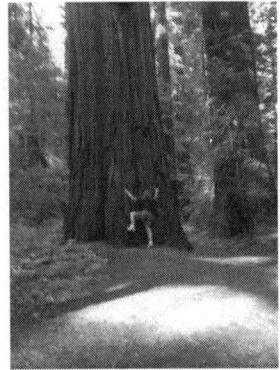

How much are we like the Redwood? We too need certain elements and conditions in order for our spirits to grow. Our spirit requires food to grow. Events in life may leave us charred like these trees, we live on.

Height is just a matter of size. It doesn't tell the dimensions of the content inside. Though I felt small as an ant, I also saw the grandeur of God's design, and with that my height soared to match that of the tallest tree. I may be short but my perspective on life is always looking up.

Points to Ponder

➤ Is your stature tall or short? Do you find your physique an issue?

➤ What makes you feel small?

➤ How are you able to overcome that feeling of smallness?

➤ The scripture says: "Nor height, nor depth, nor any other creature, shall be able to separate us from the love of God..." What does this scripture mean to you?

➤ Are you able to feed or heal your spirit through God's Word or prayer so that you are able to live on?

Challenge Yourself

❖ Stand tall amongst those things or people that make you feel small.

❖ Read God's Word and write down a scripture that helps you stand tall.

❖ Pray for someone who has made you feel small.

❖ ADD YOUR OWN CHALLENGE

November

November—Week 1

Proverbs 24:27

NRSA
Prepare your work outside, get everything ready for you in the field; and after that build your house.

KJV
Prepare thy work without, and make it fit for thyself in the field; and afterwards build thine house.

"Sometimes You Feel Like a Nut"

How many nuts could one tree hold? We have an oak tree that is dripping with acorns. After painfully stepping on and mowing over many of those pointed nuts, my husband decided a clean-up was in order. The buckets full of nuts seemed never ending. I began to think it was raining acorns—I questioned why do we need so many?

Everything has a purpose. Besides making one of the mightiest trees, the acorn provides food for wildlife, like squirrels. Feasting on these nuts, these fluffy tailed creatures stuff their mouths until they can hold no more. It's easy to understand where the term "squirreled away" comes from. The squirrel is a planner who thinks ahead, setting aside food caches to see him through the harsh, cold winter months. It's fun to watch them scurry around to bury their treasures in secret hiding places. Amazing how they know each place the nuggets are hidden.

Squirrels make different noises according to what actions they need to take; for example, if they need to defend their territory, they make one noise, or to seek food, yet another, and a different noise when they are seeking friends. My brother-in-law, Ray-Ray does a great imitation of the squirrel noises. We enjoy asking him to emulate squirrels, resulting in a lot of laughter. Until I heard these imitations, I didn't know that the squirrel has its own unique sound.

As Christians, we should take lessons from our furry, industrial friend, the squirrel. We must be ready for hard times and make noise when needed. Know when to be adventurous and when to be cautious of matters beyond our reach. We can always learn from nature, even when looking at nuts!

Points to Ponder

➤ The lesson indicates that everything has a purpose. Describe something that you believe has no purpose and why?

➤ What are the things you *squirrel away*?

➤ Why do you *squirrel away* certain things and not others?

➤ Explain why preparation is needed.

➤ Re-read the scripture. How do you prepare for the future?

➤ Does scheduling promise a future event will occur?

Challenge Yourself

❖ Take a lesson from nature and be prepared for times to come.

❖ Realize the time to be bold and the time to be guarded in life's decisions.

❖ Find other scriptures that may be helpful when you may not be prepared during hard times.

❖ ADD YOUR OWN CHALLENGE

---

2 Timothy 2:3

NRSA
Share in suffering like a good soldier of Christ Jesus.

KJV
Thou therefore endure hardness, as a good soldier of Jesus Christ.

"Unknown Soldier"

When I was eight months pregnant with our first child, my husband, Dan and I, my sister, brother-in-law, and nephew took a trip to Washington, D.C. My sister and I had been to our nation's capital when we were younger, but the others had never been. One special place we knew we wanted to revisit was the Tomb of the Unknown Soldier in Arlington National Cemetery.

The changing of the guard at the tomb was incredibly emotional! There were hundreds of visitors and yet during that moment, everyone was respectfully quiet—even reverent. The ceremony left a distinct impression of the respect displayed for this unknown veteran, who had so honorably served in the armed forces of the United States. This veteran represented those who gave the supreme sacrifice for the country. How could we not be affected?

While leaving the cemetery, the sky turned black as coal and a huge wind whipped in. The clouds burst open and within seconds, we were drenched. Then sirens sounded and people were shouting about a tornado touching down! I held my stomach and tried to run to the car. Dan told me to wait at a nearby tree. Police allowed him to drive through the cemetery to pick up his very pregnant wife.

As we left Arlington with its thousands of simple white tombstones in waves of rows across the grass, I thought of how quickly the weather had changed. I thought of those soldiers who had paid such a huge price for our freedom. I thought of how things can be one way one minute then suddenly be altered to move in another direction.

We can't predict the future or changes that blow into our lives unexpectedly. The safety we cling to is our faith. As soldiers in Christ, we owe our allegiance to one Lord and He calls us to drive closer to Him. Jesus made the supreme sacrifice for us. Would we be willing to do the same for Him?

Points to Ponder

➤ Have you or a relative served in the Armed Forces? Describe a situation of sudden danger.

➤ Have you found yourself in sudden peril? What did you do in that risky situation to ease your fear?

➤ God calls us closer to Him. What would you be willing to do for Christ? What would you be willing to do for a stranger? Should they differ?

➤ Re-read the scripture. What does it mean to be a *soldier in Christ*?

Challenge Yourself

❖ Do something special for a veteran or their family.

❖ When you face a dangerous situation, be faithful.

❖ Be willing to follow God's plan for your life.

❖ ADD YOUR OWN CHALLENGE

November—Week 3

Hebrews 1:3

NRSA
He is the reflection of God's glory and the exact imprint of God's very being, and he sustains all things by his powerful word. When he had made purification for sins, he sat down at the right hand of the Majesty on high.

KJV
Who being the brightness of his glory, and the express image of his person, and upholding all things by the word of his power, when he had by himself purged our sins, sat down on the right hand of the Majesty on high;...

"Imprints"

Autumn in Indiana is so beautiful! The trees display a vibrant array of colors. As the end of the season draws to a close, most of the leaves have fallen revealing the cold bare branches. The stark, lifeless look of the trees lets everyone know that winter is not far away.

194

Have you ever looked at leaves after they fall? The leaves retain their hue for a while before turning crisp, crunchy and brown. One day while my sister, Debby and I were leaving our parent's house, we noticed leaves had gathered in small piles on the driveway. We brushed them aside and saw leaf impressions remained even though the leaves had been removed. The leaf figure was the same shape as the leaf except void of color. It was like someone had taken an inkpad and stamped the leaves' images onto the driveway. Had I never looked at this before or had I just been too busy to notice the transferred impressions?

As we stood, transfixed by the images, I couldn't help but think of how the years pass by so quickly. I wondered how many more times we will have the chance to share a meal with our parents. We age and like the leaves, when we depart from this world, all that remains are the impressions we have made on others. Hopefully the stamp left behind is a colorful one—full of good memories. Otherwise, we will simply be brushed aside and become nothing more than dry, crumpled-up thoughts to be blown away and forgotten.

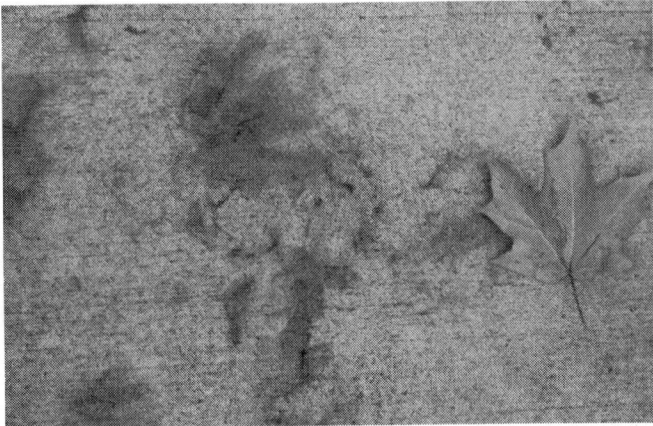

Points to Ponder

➤ Re-read the scripture. Do you think the words image and imprint mean the same thing?

➤ How would you describe the word *imprint*?

➤ What season of life best represents you right now? Describe why.

➤ Who has left their mark on your life? Do you recall when you first were aware of their impact on you?

➤ Suppose you were to pass from this life today, what imprints do you hope to leave behind?

Challenge Yourself

❖ Take a few minutes to study an imprint of something.

❖ Take a few moments to be extra patient with someone in their golden years.

❖ Write a note or telephone someone who needs encouragement.

❖ ADD YOUR OWN CHALLENGE

Philippians 4:13

NRSA
I can do all things through Him who strengthens me.

KJV
I can do all things through Christ which strengtheneth me.

"Oodles of Noodles"

To me, there is no food that feels as comforting and warms the heart like a batch of homemade noodles. Homemade noodles are a big part of our family's Thanksgiving feast. They have been a tradition for all of my life. My grandmother made them first, then my mother, and for the past several years I have had the honor of preparing the noodles. Because of our ravenous appetites for the noodles, several batches are necessary. Most years, I make so many noodles, that when I spread them out for the drying process they cover my nine-foot dining room table plus three chairs. It is a sight to behold!

One year, the venture seemed a little insurmountable because I had torn my meniscus and required arthroscopic surgery. However, not only did I need to make noodles for the feast, but Dan and I hosted the family gathering, so, I chose to postpone the surgery. Now, I could have opted to *pass the torch*, so to speak, but I really enjoy making noodles. The whole process of kneading, rolling and cutting the dough, getting flour everywhere, is really a labor of love for my family. Limping around the kitchen, I knew that making the noodles would not be my job forever...we do get older. But for now, a teaching from Philippians 4:13 spurred me on: "I can do all things through Him who strengthens me (NRSA)."

While cutting each batch, I compared my leg to a noodle. When I was little, my knees were pliable like the noodle dough. As age sets in, the knees become stiffer like the noodles after they dry out. Moving about becomes more difficult. The noodle does regain new life and flexibility when placed into boiling broth. Thankfully, the surgery on my knee had the same effect as the boiling broth did on the noodles and moving it became easier once again.

As Thanksgiving approaches, I think of the oodles of opportunities to reflect on the blessings in my life—walking pain-free and eating yummy, hot noodles will be only a few.

Points to Ponder

➢ Have you noticed, as you have aged, that your body lacks the flexibility it once had? What do you do to keep your body fit and agile?

➢ Perhaps you're inflexible not just in body, but in mind too. In your thinking, explain your flexibility or rigidity.

➢ Re-read the scripture. Have you experienced struggles in your life at inopportune times? Describe them.

➢ Were you able to *rise above* your challenges or did you succumb to them?

➢ Do you believe that you can do all things through Christ which strengthens you? Why or why not?

Challenge Yourself

❖ Pray unceasingly for God's guidance when challenges occur.

❖ When struggles do occur, rely on Christ who gives you strength. Write down your struggles and probable solutions.

❖ Think positive thoughts.

❖ ADD YOUR OWN CHALLENGE

December

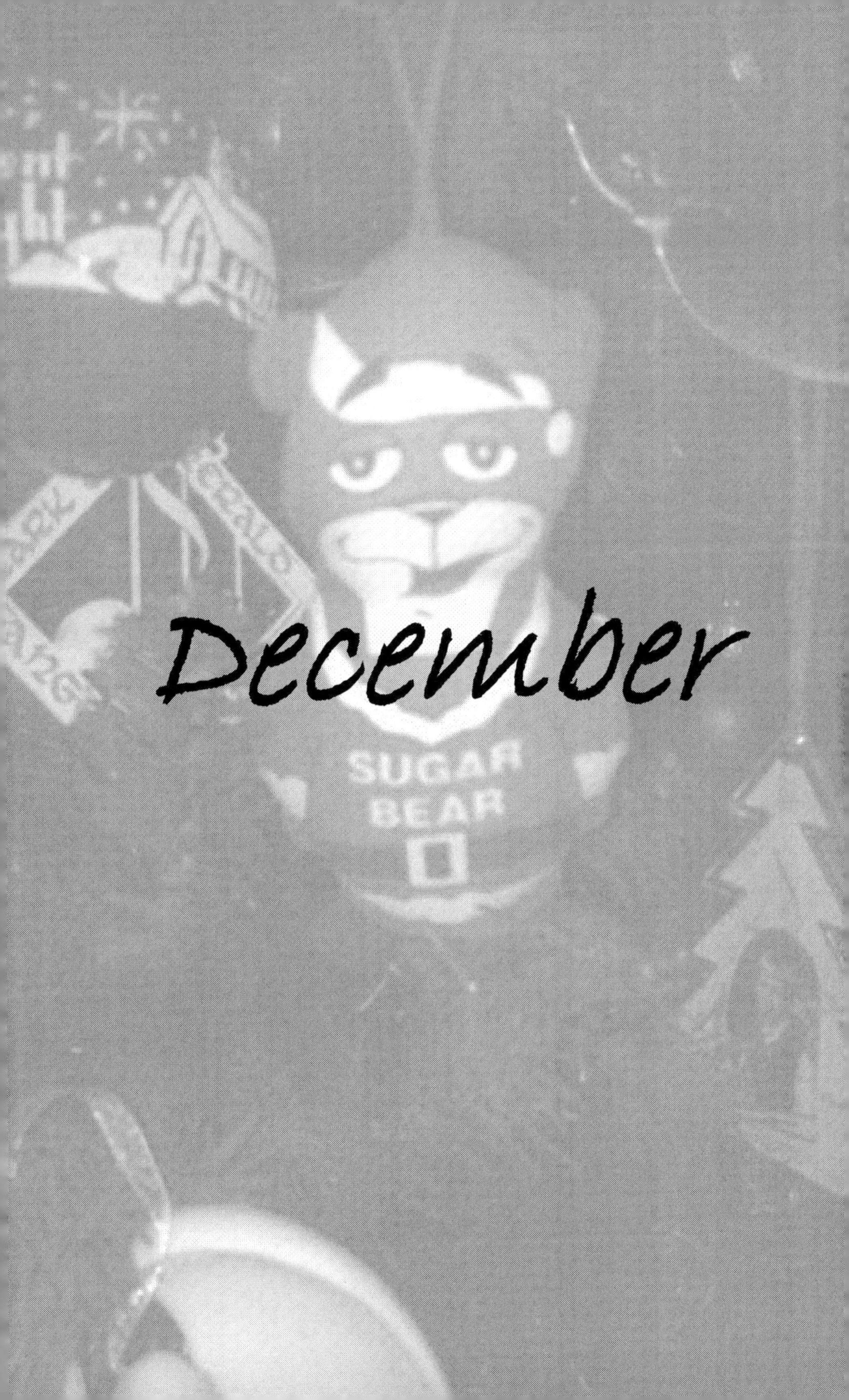

Luke 15:32

NRSA
But we had to celebrate and rejoice, because this brother of yours was dead and has come to life; he was lost and has been found.

KJV
It was meet that we should make merry, and be glad: for this thy brother was dead, and is alive again; and was lost, and is found.

"Lost and Found"

Winter can result in many things, and for me, it often leads to feeling the need to get rid of old, unused things. While the snow and cold blow outside, the closets seem to be overflowing with stuff. Mission: tackle the mess and get rid of old junk.

Sometimes treasures are found among the useless items. While unpacking a box, a Christmas tree skirt was uncovered. As I gently removed the skirt, my mind floated back in time. I had started that needlepoint item in the '80s while my children were small. It was more than half way completed, much like my life. Time does fly. I sat with the skirt in my lap and ran my fingers across the stitching. The closet light illuminated the tapestry of each knot with accents of gold and gave me pause to think, how much like this skirt am I? My life has been filled with knots that have made beautiful patterns.

At times we may feel lost, but we're really just waiting to be found. I still have many loose threads to tie together in my lifetime. I pulled the skirt out of the closet. As I resumed my stitching, I reflected, how much like the skirt we are—we are all works in progress.

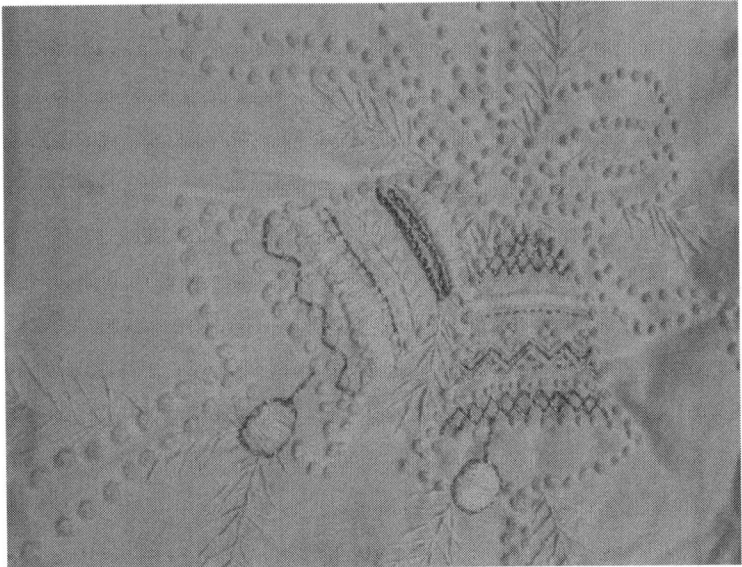

Points to Ponder

➤ Re-read the scripture. We all have put things away and thought they were lost—only to find them later. Think about one of those times and share your thoughts.

➤ Each of us has been lost, at one time or another, either when driving or walking. What were your reactions?

➤ How do you tackle a mess and face the challenge of getting rid of old things?

➤ As we live our life, changes occur. How do you deal with those changes?

➤ Do you believe that you are a work in progress? Explain.

Challenge Yourself

❖ When lost, say a prayer and God will guide the way.

❖ Rejoice in the little things.

❖ Embrace the idea that you are a work in progress.

❖ ADD YOUR OWN CHALLENGE

December—Week 2

2 Corinthians 9:7

NRSA
Each of you must give as you have made up your mind, not reluctantly or under compulsion, for God loves a cheerful giver.

KJV
Every man according as he purposeth in his heart, so let him give; not grudgingly, or of necessity: for God loveth a cheerful giver.

"Sugar Bear Returns"

One year, right before Christmas, a small package arrived in the mail. The return address was not familiar to me. What could this be? I opened the package and took out something puffy, carefully wrapped in white tissue paper. Peeling back the paper, I saw Sugar Bear! Just looking at him transported me back in time. Odd how something like that can have such a profound effect on you.

Our family tale of Sugar Bear echoed in my mind:

The Sugar Bear ornament represented a tale of siblings annoying each other. The ornament had come free in the Sugar Crisp cereal box and it played the jingle over and over again when squeezed. My middle son, Joel, would push its tummy to the point of us pleading with him to leave the ornament alone.

208

Zachary, being the oldest and definitely most musically-inclined, made many a threat to put an end to the ornament. One tree decorating time, Joel pushed the jingle beyond Zack's limits. Zachary grabbed Sugar Bear off the tree and raced into the garage. When he returned a few moments later, Zachary held the ornament over his head and with a gleam of satisfaction in his eyes declared that he had put an end to Sugar Bear. He had squeezed the song out of him by putting the ornament in his dad's vise. Zack threw it into the garbage stating that he was glad to be rid of Sugar Bear forever. We all giggled. Each of us knew Zack was frustrated, but using the vise? We were amazed by this unorthodox and out-of-character means of destruction.

I immediately took Sugar Bear out of the tissue paper, placed him on our Christmas tree and took his picture. These new phones are great because I then sent his photograph to Joel and my daughter, Brytni. They were thrilled that Sugar Bear was back on the tree. Of course, they both wanted to know where he came from. I explained that the secretary at Anderson University had mentioned, when she had read my book, *See You in a Minute, A Mother's Journey Through the First Year of Grief*, that she, too, had a Sugar Bear ornament. We both tearfully smiled at the thought of that free ornament. She had taken the time and effort to send her Sugar Bear to me.

The selflessness of others always amazes me! I'm sure that this ornament had sentimental significance to her as well, but she chose to be a giver. As we venture through the Christmas season, let us hold tight to those sugary-sweet, funny memories and remember the true spirit of the holiday. Let's choose to be generous givers and gracious, grateful receivers.

Points to Ponder

➢ Describe your favorite memory in connection to the holidays.

➢ Reflect on the holidays whether it be Christmas, Hanukkah, birthdays, and others. Which do you enjoy the most, giving or receiving gifts? Why?

➢ As it is written in the scriptures, why do you believe God loves a cheerful giver?

➢ Could you do what the secretary did and give up a beloved item just to bring joy to another? Why or not?

Challenge Yourself

❖ Hold tight to the memories, but share them with others.

❖ Be a cheerful giver.

❖ Be a gracious and grateful receiver.

❖ ADD YOUR OWN CHALLENGE

December—Week 3

Job 15:32

NRSA
It will be paid in full before their time, and their branch will not be green.

KJV
It shall be accomplished before his time, and his branch shall not be green.

"The Perfect Split"

We have a wood burning insert in our fireplace which we use to help heat our home. Log splitting usually takes place in the fall. One year, time ran short and the splitting happened in January. When Dan heard the weather forecast calling for snow and cold wintry blasts, we hauled out the log splitter and set up shop.

I did say, "We." That particular year, I helped him. It wasn't my first time, although it had been a few years. My job was working the splitter. Dan would lift the logs and I would pull the lever to make the splitter open and close. That may not sound really helpful but it speeds up the time it takes to complete the job.

The logs were a variety of sizes. Some pieces required one cut while others needed up to ten. The larger chunks were similar to slicing a huge pie. Dan would turn the log section clockwise and the splitter would slice a chunk. The pieces that had knots caused the log splitter to moan before we would hear the extremely loud "pop" of the wood breaking. As the wood was being cut, water would seep out. Dan told me that this was because the wood was still green. I found the process to be amazing!

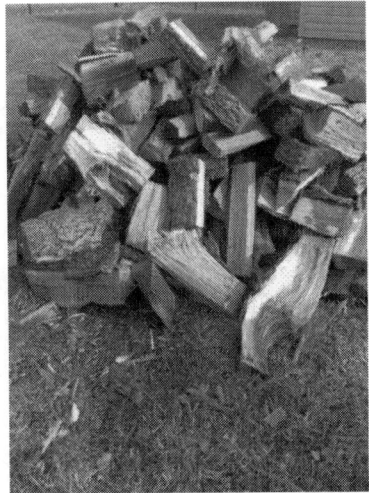

Good firewood needs to be seasoned or aged before it will burn readily. I didn't think that would make a difference, but it does. We were able to burn some of that green wood by mixing in kindling but keeping the fire going proved to be a challenge. Dan and I decided to add in more *seasoned* wood to keep the fire ablaze.

The aging of the firewood had me thinking about how the wood compares to our spiritual life. If we don't age well in the spirit, we can't burn with God's love. We need the perfect split to be on fire for the Lord. As English philosopher, Francis Bacon once said, "Age appears to be best in four things: old wood best to burn, old wine to drink, old friends to trust, and old authors to read."

Points to Ponder

➤ Do you agree with Francis Bacon's quote regarding age? Why or why not?

➤ Re-read the scripture. How is your spiritual life—is it green *new* or seasoned *old*?

➤ Have you ever been "on fire for the Lord"?

➤ Think about a time when you wished you could have helped someone accomplish a task. What stopped you?

➤ When you think about aging, what qualities come to mind? Do you think of age as a gift or a curse?

```
┌─────────────────────────────────────────┐
│            Challenge Yourself            │
│  ❖ Season your spirit to ensure you are  │
│    on fire for the Lord.                 │
│  ❖ Help someone complete a task.         │
│  ❖ Write down qualities of aging.        │
│  ❖ ADD YOUR OWN CHALLENGE                │
└─────────────────────────────────────────┘
```

2 Corinthians 1:4

NRSA
Who consoles us in all our affliction, so that we may be able to console those who are in any affliction with the consolation with which we ourselves are consoled by God.

KJV
Who comforteth us in all our tribulation, that we may be able to comfort them which are in any trouble, by the comfort wherewith we ourselves are comforted of God.

"Finding Comfort from the Winter Chill"

A warm, cozy fire on a cold evening—it warms the body and the soul. I feel blessed that my husband works hard all year preparing for bitter cold winter nights. Throughout the year, he searches for trees that need to be chopped down, splits, hauls and stacks the wood. Our beautiful, glowing fire didn't just magically happen. It is the direct result of a lot of manual labor. The beauty of our fire reflects his effort...his labor of love.

The season of Christmas doesn't always result in the same emotions as the warmth of a fire. My heart is heavy thinking of those who are in pain during this season. It is difficult when someone is hurting to find a place of peace and comfort. I pray that they can find a fire to warm their spirit.

During this holiday season, seek to find warmth somewhere—whether it is in the laughter of a small child, the smile of a grandparent, the glow in the eyes of a loved one, or a "Merry Christmas" from someone passing by. Look for the small, special moments that happen each day.

Life is like a cozy, warm fire. The best results don't come without a lot of searching, preparing and effort. Let's all strive to build a fire for others to enjoy!

Points to Ponder

➤ Describe something you work hard for all year and appreciate later.

➤ Re-read the scripture. What do you find gives you comfort?

➤ Do you know people in pain during the holiday season? Describe what you could do to comfort those people.

➤ Have you ever avoided helping others because you thought it would take too much work or time? Explain the event.

➤ Realizing that nothing happens without a little preparing and effort, explain how you will provide peace and comfort to another.

Challenge Yourself

❖ Give your time or talent to comfort someone in need.

❖ Look for special moments each day.

❖ Appreciate that hard work brings comfort to you and others.

❖ ADD YOUR OWN CHALLENGE

WITH GOD
ALL THINGS

Added
Spice

POSSIBLE.

Ezekiel 44:23

NRSA
They shall teach my people the difference between the holy and the common, and show them how to distinguish between the unclean and the clean.

KJV
And they shall teach my people the difference between the holy and profane, and cause them to discern between the unclean and the clean.

"Father Knows Best"

When I was a little girl, I loved certain television shows. Most of them were in black and white. Color wasn't an issue. The plot and the characters were the things that kept me tuning in each week.

Some of those classics can still be viewed today on the retro stations. Lately, I've been watching them again. "Father Knows Best" is one. I find myself retaining the moral message each episode illustrates and even sharing it with others. Occasionally, a show may leave me a little teary-eyed but I still walk away feeling spiritually uplifted.

These classic shows are very different in that they never contain sexual innuendoes or cussing. I find that refreshing! The Anderson's are just a middle class family working together to make it through life. Granted their attires and hairstyles aren't current, but the messages are still clearly up-to-date. They struggle to find truth, love, and happiness; just as we all do today.

Each of us wants to feel good inside and out. It is up to us to take into our spirits things that boost us up and not fill us with festering junk. It's up to us to choose wisely what comes into our head and heart. We need to pray and ask our Lord for guidance and strength. After all, it's true that our Heavenly Father really does know us best!

Points to Ponder

➤ What old shows still resonate with you?

➤ Have you ever watched a show that made you feel uncomfortable or even a little sick inside? Explain.

➤ Read the scripture about wisdom aloud. Discuss its meaning and how it applies to the term, *Father*.

➤ What can you do instead of taking in thoughts that are not good for your spirit?

➤ Think back to childhood or youth. How did you connect with God?

Challenge Yourself

❖ Turn off the television and connect with Our Lord.

❖ Make an effort to avoid things that bring you down spiritually.

❖ Write down a scripture and memorize it.

❖ ADD YOUR OWN CHALLENGE

Proverbs 3:6-8

NRSA

6 In all your ways acknowledge him, and he will make straight your paths. 7 Do not be wise in your own eyes; fear the Lord, and turn away from evil. 8 It will be a healing for your flesh and a refreshment for your body.

KJV

6 In all thy ways acknowledge him, and he shall direct thy paths. 7 Be not wise in thine own eyes: fear the LORD, and depart from evil. 8 It shall be health to thy navel, and marrow to thy bones.

"Hoping for Healing"

Have you ever been so sick that just standing up was an effort or walking seemed an insurmountable task or raising your head felt like lifting a humongous boulder? That was me not too long ago.

As I lay in bed, I hoped to just make it through to the next day. Then, on the third day of experiencing that nasty flu bug, there was a light at the end of the tunnel. It was on the evening of that third day that I thought of those who experience deep sickness...sickness that lasts longer than a mere three days. In my heart, even when my head was pounding and my stomach felt more than a little uneasy, I knew that this achy feeling would pass eventually. What about those who are unsure of the next day? What about those who have cancer or those who have had a stroke or those who have had a heart attack or other dreaded circumstances?

That horrible flu taught me a thoughtful lesson. Even in the depths of illness when it feels like an alien has invaded your body and taken control, somebody has it worse. Someone is spending their days in a hospital or nursing home or somewhere trying to hold their head up and move toward the next minute, next hour, next day, next week, next month...the next year.

Let us cherish the moments of good health and pray for those who are in need. We can send words of encouragement, cards or packages to help lighten the burden. If we can't help physically, we can always pray. Healing does not begin or end with us. Let's help heal the spirits of those around us!

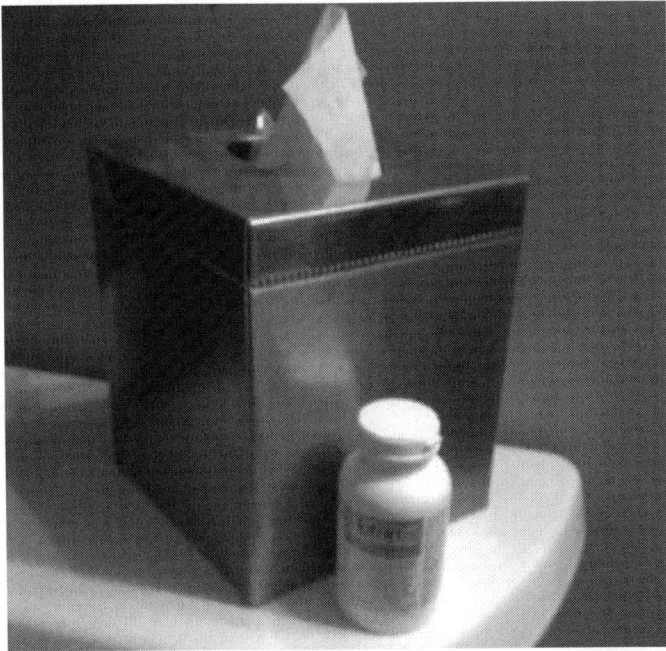

Points to Ponder

- Describe your attitude concerning health and fitness.

- Describe a time when you were ill. Did it seem never-ending?

- Recount a situation when you reached out to another person who was not well. What did you do?

- Re-read the scripture. Do you believe in the power of prayer for healing? Why or why not?

- Have you witnessed another person's healing by the power of prayer? Explain.

Challenge Yourself

- Get fit, physically and spiritually.

- Be thoughtful of others when they are ill by reaching out with a card or words of encouragement.

- Pray and believe for healing for yourself and others.

- ADD YOUR OWN CHALLENGE

Month 3—Week 5

Ephesians 4:32

NRSA
And be kind to one another, tenderhearted, forgiving one another, as God in Christ has forgiven you

KJV
And be ye kind one to another, tenderhearted, forgiving one another, even as God for Christ's sake hath forgiven you.

"It's About Forgiveness"

To forgive—it's more than just a word. It's a profound and often emotional action. "Forgive" means to wipe the slate clean, to pardon, and to cancel a debt. That sounds reasonable but can feel overwhelming. When you have been hurt, cut to your heart, how easily is that slate wiped clean?

We have all been hurt and have hurt another person. When you love someone, there is bound to be damage. The Bible gives us much instruction when it comes to forgiveness. Forgiveness is not granted because a person deserves to be forgiven. Instead, it is an act of love, mercy, and grace.

Easter is a holiday celebrating our Lord's Passion and resurrection. At our church, the cross is wrapped in crimson red which represents the blood Jesus shed for our sins. It remains covered until Easter Sunday. When I think about the Lord's death on the cross when He asked, "Father, forgive them, for they know not what they do," I am speechless. All the abuse and torture He endured for all of us is unfathomable. This clothed cross is such a powerful visual reminder of His sacrifice and forgiveness.

The arguments and hurt feelings we endure are minuscule next to Jesus' torturous path. We must let go and let God touch our hearts to release the burden of the hurt in our lives. The actor, Tyler Perry said, "It's not an easy journey, to get to a place where you forgive people. But it is such a powerful place, because it frees you." Let us rise with our Lord and celebrate forgiveness. Only then can we be free to love...and live.

Points to Ponder

➤ What does the Bible say about forgiveness? (Luke 6:37, 1 John 1:9-10, Matthew 26:28)

➤ Have you ever held a grudge? Explain.

➤ If you forgive someone, do you truly let go of the hurt or do you continue to hold it inside you?

➤ Reread Tyler Perry's quote aloud. Do you agree or disagree with his thoughts?

➤ Study the pictures of the cross. Discuss the meaning behind those photographs.

Challenge Yourself

❖ Forgive anyone who has hurt you.

❖ Reflect on the message of the cross and take it all in.

❖ ADD YOUR OWN CHALLENGE

Month 4—Week 5

Matthew 8:20

NRSA
And Jesus said to him, "Foxes have holes, and birds of the air have nests; but the Son of Man has nowhere to lay his head."

KJV
And Jesus saith unto him, the foxes have holes, and the birds of the air have nests; but the Son of man hath not where to lay his head.

"Make Way for Ducks"

One day, I arose around sunrise and decided to get in an early morning walk. Heading down the driveway, I was startled to see a couple of Mallard ducks standing in the street. Fascinated by their appearance, I quickly began snapping their picture. Not living near a lake, I was surprised to see them in my neighborhood.

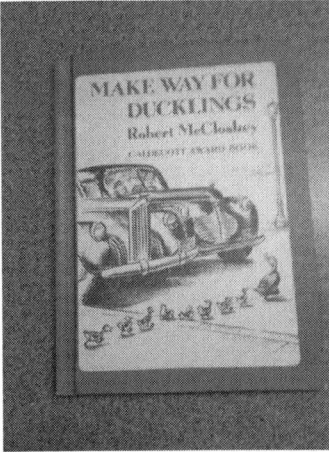

The sight made me think about a story I loved as child entitled, *Make Way for Ducklings* by Robert McCloskey. The book tells the story of a Mr. and Mrs. Mallard who decide to raise their family in a park in the center of Boston. The couple endures many trials due to this decision, but, with the help of some concerned people, the story has a happy ending. As I clicked pictures of these two ducks waddling across the yard, I couldn't help but make connections between the ducks in the story and these two characters. Why were they in this location? Were they lost? Would they depend on us to help them if they stayed? I walked on but continued to think about this feathered couple.

Returning from my morning walk, Mr. and Mrs. Mallard must have decided that this was not the place to settle down. I only looked for them for a few minutes but felt relieved that this had not become their final destination. Our front yard wasn't suitable as a home for ducks!

Sometimes we, too, find ourselves out of our element, much like a *duck out of water*. In times like these, it is more important than ever to seek The Lord for answers. It is knowing that He will be there for us, guiding our way, that allows us to reach our final destination.

Points to Ponder

➢ When you see something out of place, how do you react?

➢ When have you felt like a *duck out of water?*

➢ What childhood book has left an impression on you? Did it involve animals as well?

➢ Re-read the scripture. Where do you think that God can be seen?

➢ Describe conflicts you have when approaching the unknown.

Challenge Yourself

❖ Take a walk in nature and reflect on how God is present.

❖ Be kind to someone who may feel out of place.

❖ ADD YOUR OWN CHALLENGE

Made in the USA
Lexington, KY
29 February 2016